Trip first

3 beds
call paul

All my x's are
from Texas

R u sure u want a Texan
accent to rub off on you?

Read proverbs in making your
decision

The Heat

When in t world was mary
in Texas? where was I?

Not Just snakes but poisonous ones

Please Don't SQUEEZE THE CHRISTIAN

Into the World's Mold

Scott Sernau

INTERVARSITY PRESS
DOWNERS GROVE, ILLINOIS 60515

Acknowledgments

The song on page 91 is from "My Little Town," Copyright © 1975. Used by permission.

The poem on page 105 is from "The Hollow Men" in COLLECTED POEMS 1909-1962 by T. S. Eliot, copyright 1936 by Harcourt Brace Jovanovich, Inc.; copyright © 1963, 1964 by T. S. Eliot. Reprinted by permission of the publisher.

InterVarsity Press is the book-publishing division of InterVarsity Christian Fellowship, a student movement active on campus at hundreds of universities, colleges and schools of nursing. For information about local and regional activities, write Public Relations Dept., InterVarsity Christian Fellowship, 6400 Schroeder Rd., P.O. Box 7895, Madison, WI 53707-7895.

Distributed in Canada through InterVarsity Press, 860 Denison St., Unit 3, Markham, Ontario L3R 4H1, Canada.

All Scripture quotations, unless otherwise indicated, are from the Holy Bible, New International Version. Copyright © 1973, 1978, International Bible Society. Used by permission of Zondervan Bible Publishers.

Cover illustration: Joe DeVelasco

ISBN 0-87784-571-9

Printed in the United States of America

Library of Congress Cataloging-in-Publication Data

Sernau, Scott.
  Please don't squeeze the Christian into the world's mold.

  Bibliography: p.
  1. Christianity and culture.   2. Christian life—
1960-   .   I. Title.
BR115.C8S47   1987   261   87-3155
ISBN 0-87784-571-9

17	16	15	14	13	12	11	10	9	8	7	6	5	4	3	2	1
99	98	97	96	95	94	93	92	91	90	89	88	87				

Preface

SQUEEZED.

That's how it feels sometimes. Squeezed in by life, by the world around us. Dozens of voices tell us what we should do, wear, buy—what we should be. Demands and pressures come from all sides calling us to conform, shape up, get in line, get in step. Amidst that jumble of voices, it's easy to feel confused about who we are and about *whose* we are.

This is an invitation to step back in order to examine where we're headed and to make choices. To examine the world in which we live and its demands, to listen for a higher calling, to decide about our own lives. The questions I ask are not rhetorical. Answer them for your own life. That's why this is a small book on a big topic—the rest is up to you to write as you work out the applications in your life.

Don't read the suggestions which complete each chapter as lists of "ought to's," but as pointers to help you begin the process of cutting the cords of conformity. These can be the first steps out of the miry ways of the world and a path to higher ground. The chapters are not isolated but facets of a single pattern, and so they intentionally restate shared ideas (a fine Hebrew tradition). We don't need rigid codes calling for further conformity but paths toward wholehearted living for whole people. And this is what we find in joyfully responding to the transforming touch of our loving Lord: the adventurous, contagious life of faith set free.

Remember, you're not the person you once were. None of us are. Every day and every moment we make choices, and those choices change us. They determine who we are becoming and where we are heading. Yes, you're being conformed to a mold, but the good news is that you can choose that mold. Will you be an assembly-line copy of our society, one more voice in the crowd? Or will you be a unique creation of the Master Craftsman, a setting for his good news, a setting cast in the Master's mold?

WELCOME
TO THE
WORLD

1

Civilization is coming to an end!
Children no longer respect their parents. Violence and
strife are everywhere. Our values are gone.
ANCIENT BABYLONIAN INSCRIPTION

CONCERN ABOUT OUR WORLD IS NOTHING NEW. SINCE THE DAWN of civilization people have looked at their society and shaken their heads. In response some have become either hermits or revolutionaries, cynics or martyrs. Some look longingly back to the "good old days" and mutter about what the world is coming to. Others look to the future, confident that once their plan is implemented or their candidate is in power, then everything will be perfect. Still others simply shake their heads in confusion and wonder, "What's going on out there?"

But that is our error. The world is not something going on "out there." Since the day we were born, the world has been molding our attitudes, our thinking, our ethics, our aspirations and our activities. As much as we would like to think of ourselves as "our own person," we must confess that even this desire has been cultivated by the values of our culture. <u>We are all children of our times.</u>

We see this clearly when we look at values in other times and places. If we were able to resurrect an ancient Greek Spartan and have him interviewed by the next pollster who came to our door, our pollster might be in for quite a surprise:

"Your name?"

"Achilles Helios."

"Age?"

"2500 years."

"Home?"

"Sparta."

"Fine. Now tell me, Mr. Helios, what is your position on youth and the military draft?"

"Simple. When my son left for the wars, I said that I wanted to hear news of his victories or news of his death. I told him, 'Come back with your shield or come back on your shield.' "

"How do you perceive the problem of the separation of church and state?"

"No problem. Insubordination to the gods of Sparta is insubordination to the state of Sparta. If someone won't sacrifice to the gods, let him *be* sacrificed to the gods."

"What is your view of the prospects for peaceful negotiation of international differences?"

"The only way to make a lasting point is with the point of a javelin. It's best to negotiate with a foe after you've run a phalanx over him—he argues less that way."

"What do you see as the primary obstacle to effective government?"

"Democracy. An invention of idlers who wanted a stage on which to spew forth their foolishness. Progress demands the strong hand of a dictator—always has, always will."

"Who do you feel is responsible for the economic problem?"

"Slaves. They're not being dealt with with a stern enough hand, and so they're becoming nonproductive. They're drawn from inferior peoples, and so of course they must be prodded and directed."

To us Achilles seems militaristic, calloused, superstitious and cruel. We might condemn him for his blindness to the injustices of slavery and tyranny, and marvel at his scorn of democracy and peace. We've come a long way. But Achilles would likely see things differently. If we asked him for his impressions of our society, he might respond: "I'm shocked at your lack of respect for authority, your irreverence, your indolence and utter lack of discipline, your self-centeredness and complete lack of any sense of duty. Have you no pride?"

Disgust would likely be his response to our lack of courage and strength of character: "A decrepit society without values, standing for nothing and going nowhere. I doubt there's a man among you."

Now I'm not suggesting that we all wholeheartedly revert back to the norms of ancient Sparta. Our problem is not that we are modern. The problem has been around at least as long as the complaint of the ancient Babylonian which began this chapter. Rather, our problem has to do with "the world."

Our Spartan would have made a distinction between *ge*, the physical earth (from which we get *geology*) and *kosmos*, the world. He might use *kosmos* to refer simply to all of humanity ("all the world"), but the word has its roots in the idea of order, pattern, arrangement: "the way of the world." Likewise, when the New Testament writers warn us of the world (*kosmos*), their concern is that we not blindly conform to the pattern of our age.

As one who was too close for comfort when Mt. St. Helens blew off some steam, I assure you that the dangers of the *ge* are often loud and highly visible. The dangers of the *kosmos*, on the other hand, are rarely so. They work from the inside out. Remember the story of the man who wore an iron mask until his face finally conformed to fit it? We shake our heads at the cruelty of our ancestors—until we read today's newspaper. We're amazed at the way Communist peoples are molded by state propaganda. We marvel at the bigotry, petty rivalries, inbred hatreds and vengefulness of people in foreign trouble spots—all the while ignoring our own.

The pattern of our age, our society, our culture, forms the glasses through which we see and bring things into focus. But what if those glasses are bent out of shape? The man who needs thick spectacles to see can never remove and inspect them. Clearly he needs the assistance of a friend.

Eugene Peterson describes the problem this way:

World is an atmosphere, a mood. It is nearly as hard for a sinner to recognize the world's temptations as it is for a fish to discover impurities in the water. There is a sense, a feeling, that things aren't right, that the environment is not whole, but just what it is eludes analysis. We know that the spiritual atmosphere in which we live erodes faith, dissipates hope and corrupts love, but it is hard to put our finger on what is wrong.[1]

Like the ancient Babylonian, we know something is desperately wrong with our world, but we can't get a handle on it. We see the world forcing us into its mold and we want to break out, but we don't know how. We want to affirm faith, hope and love, but they've become elusive terms. We want to live lives of excellence, but in pursuing that goal we stumble over the complicated clutter and trash of our complicated day. We long for stronger, more vibrant and meaningful lives, but our everyday world is all we've ever known. We can't see our blind spots for the very reason that we're blind. What then can we do?

We need a broader perspective—to step out of our cultural limitations. We need a deeper perspective—to step out of our historical limitations. And we need a higher perspective—to step out of our narrow, human limitations. To see beyond the limits of our world we need the help of one whose roots are not in this world. Only one man can help.

The Man from Nazareth

Let's face it: Jesus grew up in a bad neighborhood. Galilee had never been a very healthy place for a good Jewish boy. A constant crossroads of diverse peoples, it had been the first place to set up altars to foreign gods and the first place to be invaded. It hadn't been truly Jewish since Shalmaneser of Assyria had paid an uninvited visit some seven centuries earlier. Now under Roman domination and Greek influence, it was truly "Galilee of the Gentiles," and many pious Jews down south in the Bible Belt around Jerusalem scarcely considered it to be Jewish territory. It had succumbed to the world.

Syria, immediately to the north, was thoroughly Hellenized and the center of Roman authority. Only a few miles from Nazareth were Greek communities, and on the Sea of Galilee was a new Roman town. Not that Nazareth itself proved much better than these. It was considered so corrupt that pious Jews could only ask, "Can anything good come out of Nazareth?" Still these Jews had to admit that even Judea itself was no longer a good Jewish nation. For three hundred years it had been under Greek influence, and now it had fallen under Roman domination. In Jerusalem a Roman fortress abutted the Temple itself, and right down the street were theaters and coliseums. Faced with these corrupting influences, the Jews were rudely confronted by the world. Men of conscience had to take a stand.

Some became Zealots. They hid daggers in their cloaks, threatened violence and longed for a fight that would "purify" their nation. Others joined the Essenes. They wore white, espoused a mystical theology and longed for deliverance from the world through the soon-expected coming of God's kingdom. They rejected the Temple and Jerusalem as defiled, and when they could, they retreated to isolated communes (such as Qumran, where the Dead Sea Scrolls were found).

More significant, however, were those who followed the teachings of the Sadducees and Pharisees. The Sadducees were men of the world. Many were clergy, but they were also men of wealth and position. To them the best course was to look as much like the surrounding world as possible. If they conformed, at least the Romans wouldn't come and take away their "place" (Jn 11:48—that is, their places of prestige and respect). When under Rome, do as the Romans do. God helps those who help themselves.

The Pharisees, on the other hand, were the separated ones. They knew the hazards of pagan culture, and so they spent their days expanding and refining their lists of "thou shalt nots." To make sure that no one even inadvertently transgressed the Law, they constructed elaborate regulations so that anything that even resembled worldliness could be avoided. They were men of deep conviction, and they wore their laws in boxes on their foreheads and sleeves so that everyone knew it.

It was into this confusion of how to deal with a world gone wrong that Jesus, the teacher from Nazareth, came. Many of the questions leveled at him were attempts to force him to declare his loyalties—to which of these groups did he belong? What was his solution to Roman rule? Would he forbid paying taxes? Would he declare war on Rome? Lead a revolt? Would he lead his followers into the desert? Start a commune? Would he allow himself to be crowned king? Would he try to do away with the Jewish Law? Would he seek to make the Law even more complex?

To their consternation, Jesus did none of these things. People tried to make him the champion of their own causes and campaigns (as they still do), but he refused to be pressed into an old mold. He warned that any that tried to force his new wine into old wineskins would find those skins bursting. He came neither to conform to the world, nor to condemn it. He came to transform the world, to usher in a new world, a "third way," the kingdom of God.

To those who flared with zealous anger, Jesus warned that all who take the sword die by the sword, and reminded them that his kingdom was not of this world. To those in sympathy with the reclusive Essenes, he challenged them to become the salt of the earth, the light of the world which cannot be hidden. He beckoned them to let the quality of their lives shine before others, glorifying their Father in heaven. Confronted by the Sadducees, he warned them that they were in error because they knew neither the Scriptures nor the power of God.

Challenged by the Pharisees, he warned them that they were setting aside the commandments of God (the very commandments they treasured) in order to keep their traditions. He called them hypocrites. He said that in their attempt at purity, they had become whitewashed tombs: pure and white on the outside, but full of death inside.

It's ironic (though given human nature, perhaps not surprising) that many who in some way acknowledge Jesus today fall into the same camps as those Jesus faced. We have our groups of zealots, like the KKK and New Aryans. We also have a proliferation of cults and communes hiding in the hills waiting for the day of reckoning.

But mostly we have modern Pharisees and Sadducees. Modern Sadducees do things "right": they drive the right cars, wear the right clothes and espouse the right ideals. Yes they believe in God and country, but religion is equated with decency and propriety. It keeps things safe for the status quo. "God helps those who help themselves."

Modern Pharisees make a point of remaining separated. Careful not to be seen with sinners and publicans, they avoid dealing with the world, move in "holy huddles" and carry extensive lists of "thou shalt nots." They don't "smoke, drink or chew, or go with girls who do." They've worked hard to become humble servants of God, and they're proud of it.

To the Sadducees, Jesus warns that propriety is not godliness, and self-sufficiency can be deadly when one knows neither the Scriptures nor the power of God. To the Pharisees, Jesus warns that negativism is not holiness, and that spiritual pride is a cancer that kills from within, leaving whitewashed tombs.

Both groups are undeniably religious, but remember that the

original Pharisees and Sadducees agreed on one thing: their religious systems had no room for this certain Jesus, called the Christ.

The Third Way

Jesus refused to play the part of either an activist or a passivist, a conformist or a rebel, a liberal or a conservative. For what he brought was not reformation but transformation; he was instituting a whole new way of life.

Neither condemning nor conforming, Jesus revolutionized his world. Everywhere he went he preached the good news of the kingdom of God. "What are the rules of this kingdom?" lawyers wanted to know. Jesus answered, "Love the Lord your God with all your heart and with all your soul and with all your mind and with all your strength." And " 'You shall love your neighbor as yourself.' There is no commandment greater than these" (Mk 12:30-31). What was revolutionary was not that Jesus said these two commandments—they are quotes from the Old Testament Law and some of the Pharisees listening may well have been wearing those words on their sleeves (literally)—but that he lived them.

Everywhere he went, Jesus transformed people no matter what their background or culture. Jews flocked to hear him teaching as one with authority and to be healed. Greeks came pleading, "We want to see Jesus." People of Samaria and Phoenicia were moved to faith, and even Roman military commanders were awed by his character and authority. He brought a message of faith, hope and love, and lives were transformed. Truly Peter confessed, "Master, you have the words of life." Those few who remained beside him—that motley crew from the bad part of town—became those "who have turned the world upside down" (Acts 17:6 RSV). They were molded by his teaching, his example and, above all, by his Spirit. That's transformation! The world couldn't understand what had happened to these simple, unlearned people, and then it was reported, "They had been with Jesus" (Acts 4:13 RSV). And that alone made all the difference.

At this point you may be thinking, "Yes I remember my Sunday-school lessons, but it's a different world out there today. Complicated, confused, cluttered, clamoring, changing—how can I take those words, two millennia old, and make them real today?" Surprisingly, our best insights into this task are ancient themselves, and they come from a man who once was "as to the law, a *Pharisee.*"

The Pharisee from Tarsus

The apostle Paul was a cultural schizophrenic. He was born in Greek-speaking Tarsus of Hebrew parents who were Roman citizens. Multilingual and trained in the literature of several cultures, Paul found his identity in being "of the tribe of Benjamin, a Hebrew of Hebrews; in regard to the law, a Pharisee; as for zeal, persecuting the church; as for legalistic righteousness, faultless" (Phil 3:5-6). But after he encountered Jesus for himself, he came to "consider everything a loss compared to the surpassing greatness of knowing Christ Jesus my Lord, for whose sake I have lost all things. I consider them rubbish, that I may gain Christ" (Phil 3:8). Paul's message as he faced the world became, "Everything that separates us from Christ is junk."

In calling his world to Christ, Paul continually came up against the patterns of his age. He faced both Judaizers, who equated godliness with Jewish ritual, and Hellenizers, who equated godliness with Greek mysticism. Paul argued in both the synagogues with Jews and the marketplaces with Greeks. His letter to the Colossians, written to a churcn at just one of these cultural crossroads, is the classic manual on dealing with the problems of the world. Against the Judaizers Paul warns, "Do not let anyone judge you by what you eat or drink, or with regard to a religious festival, a New Moon celebration or a Sabbath day. These are a shadow of the things that were to come; the reality, however, is found in Christ" (Col 2:16-17).

And against the mystics he warns:

Do not let anyone who delights in false humility and the worship of angels disqualify you for the prize. Such a person goes into great detail about what he has seen, and his unspiritual mind puffs him up with idle notions. He has lost connection with the Head, from whom the whole body, supported and held together by its ligaments and sinews, grows as God causes it to grow. (Col 2:18-19)

These ways of combating the world, Paul claims, are in fact worldly themselves:

Since you died with Christ to the basic principles of this world, why, as though you still belonged to it, do you submit to its rules: "Do not handle! Do not taste! Do not touch!"? . . . Such regulations indeed have an appearance of wisdom, with their self-imposed worship, their false humility and their harsh treatment of the body, but they lack any value in restraining sensual indulgence. (Col 2:20-23)

This battle requires different tactics, as he had written earlier to the Corinthians:

I beg you that when I come I may not have to be as bold as I expect to be toward some people who think that we live by the standards of this world. For though we live in the world, we do not wage war as the world does. The weapons we fight with are not the weapons of the world. On the contrary, they have divine power to demolish strongholds. We demolish arguments and every pretension that sets itself up against the knowledge of God, and we take captive every thought to make it obedient to Christ, (2 Cor 10:2-5)

Paul summarizes this in a comprehensive warning: "See to it that no one takes you captive through hollow and deceptive philosophy, which depends on human tradition and the basic principles of this world rather than on Christ" (Col 2:8).

To the Judaizers all of the non-Jewish world were uncircumcised Gentile dogs, and to the Hellenizers all of the non-Greek world were uncivilized barbarians. Their solution to the problem of the world was one still used today: "Make them all like us." One side wanted everyone to be Jews; the other wanted all to be Greeks. Paul's response is to remind them of the character of Christ's new kingdom, "Here there is no Greek or Jew, circumcised or uncircumcised, barbarian, Scythian, slave or free, but Christ is all, and is in all" (Col 3:11).

This is where we must begin today. As Leo Tolstoy wrote: "Everybody thinks of changing the world and nobody thinks of changing himself." Paul's solution is simple (but not easy): "Do not conform any longer to the pattern of this world, but be transformed by the renewing of your mind" (Rom 12:2). The Phillips translation phrases it, "Don't let the world around you squeeze you into its mould, but let God re-make you so that your whole attitude of mind is changed." To avoid this squeeze, we must be transformed. The Greek word here is *metamorphousthe*; like a caterpillar being transformed into a butterfly, we need to be metamorphosed.

It is natural that at times we feel crowded by our world and its demands. "We cannot avoid being in crowds. Can we keep from being crowd-conditioned? Can we keep from trading our name in for a number, from letting the crowd reduce us to mindless passivity?"[2] The answer to these questions is only affirmative when our minds are renewed by the man from Nazareth, who immersed himself in crowds and yet remained true to his calling. The slow, deep transformation he brings is still the only true, lasting revolution.

Just as the pressure to conform is a constant process, so the renewal of our minds must be a constant process. Every moment we are being molded. The only question is, Who's mold? They say that in time dogs begin to look like their masters. I don't know if that is really true of dogs (although I can think of a few examples), but I'm sure it's true of people. In time we come to look like our masters. If we blindly follow the patterns of our world, we will constantly come to look more and more like our world. But if in all things we look to the one we call Lord and Master, then we shall begin to take on his likeness. It's a slow process, but we're promised its completion.

This book is about transformation. By studying the trends of our times, we will explore what it means to be transformed rather than conformed. Also, we will look to see how we can be active transformers of our world, to see how we can have an impact on our age, becoming healers to a hurting world.

I believe we can again "turn the world upside down," not with loud movements, but with the quiet strength of inner integrity. Paul gives us an exciting yet somber challenge by calling us to live as "faultless children of God, living in a warped and diseased age, and shining like lights in a dark world" (Phil 2:15 Phillips).

THE
JUNK
GENERATION

LIVING IN AN AGE OF SUPERFICIALITY

2

You can't do anything about the length of your life, but you can do something about its width and depth.

H. L. MENCKEN

SPACE AGE. ELECTRONIC AGE. ATOMIC AGE.

These are titles we give to our times, and they sound impressive. They speak of the power of technology. But future archaeologists digging through our rubble may well have another name for us—"The Junk Age." Junk is the product, as well as the by-product, of mass production and mass consumption. Quality becomes lost in a plethora of quantity.

Fast, Cheap, Trivial, Disposable

What am I calling junk? It has four qualities. First, it's fast: instant coffee, overnight successes and condensed Bibles. Our lives have become a desperate war on time, and if quality and value are among the casualties, then so be it.

Second, junk is cheap: life is short so we must "grab for all the gusto" we can get. To work for anything is a waste of precious time and effort since everything can easily be replaced by something else.

Third, it's trivial: when our lives are filled with a blur of passing objects, events, ideas and people, we can't afford to attach much meaning or value to any of them.

Finally, it is disposable. Why not? If it's cheap and trivial and there's something new just around the corner, then it's foolish sentimentality to hang on to the old.

We're all familiar with junk food. It's fast and cheap and comes in disposable packages, lurking under layers of paper and Styrofoam. If you have hesitations, loud and persistent advertising will drown them. After all, as Bruce Lockerbie asked, "Could 25 Billion Hamburgers Be Wrong?"[1]

Junk, however, is not limited to food: it permeates our lives. We want all that Madison Avenue offers, and if we can't afford it (as most of us can't), then we'll sacrifice quality rather than quantity. We fill our closets with the latest "bargains," our shelves with the latest trinkets, and our counters with the latest appliances. Who needs a stove when you can have an electric wok and a popcorn popper with "power shakes"? And why worry when your wok won't work and the "power shakes" breaks? The glossy on your doorstep offers something better, on sale today!

Perhaps even more pervasive than material junk is cultural junk. The average person used to have one or two pieces of fine art as a keepsake; today we can fill our homes with Oriental "art," courtesy of Hong Kong. People once had only a few good books; today's classics come in prepackaged series and genre. Today's best-selling writers can crank out a blockbuster a month—Shakespeare would be chagrined! Perhaps they all sound a bit alike, but you're getting more page per penny. Why grapple with the slow, difficult oldies when right at the check-out stand for only 45¢, a top psychic will tell you, in a single column, how to lose weight overnight with a diet suited to your astrological sign? With the largest circulation in the country, would they lie?

Only on special occasions did people once go to see a play. Now we absorb an average of seven hours of network drama a day. Of course no writer of a series can produce consistent quality at twenty-six episodes per year, but who cares if the stars' lines are flat as long as their figures aren't? People complain, but they still watch, and watch, and watch. Music was once a special event; now it drones through our every minute. Music producers hear a different tune: there's an incredible market out there, so ignore art—packaging and production are what count. Today's hit is tomorrow's moldy oldie. Sure the lyrics reek, but the promo is slick, and besides, she'll have a new hit next week. So media electronic glitter becomes mere electronic litter.

Disposable Relationships and People

Junk doesn't stop with culture. Take a look at today's relationships and the trend becomes clear. Junk relationships abound: they're fast, cheap, trivial and ultimately disposable.

Friendliness becomes junk when a helping hand becomes a "Have a Nice Day" button. Cheerfulness in the public eye is expected today, but cheerfulness is no substitute for love anymore than a candy bar is a substitute for a meal—and those who try to live on it are bound to suffer emotional malnutrition.

Junk laughter begins in tinselly frivolity and ends in cynical sarcasm. Junk caring says, "I'm OK, you're OK, so why sweat it?"

Junk romance is instant intimacy. It's Olivia Newton-John's "Physical": after one evening of talking, they know all there is that's worth knowing about each other, and so there's nothing left but to "get physical." Ah, but they didn't warn her: junk relationships bring junk sex.

And junk marriage? We decry the divorce rate, but when the process is fast, the investment is cheap and the vows are trivial, why shouldn't the result be disposable? Look at the wedding presents: when the wok wouldn't work and the popcorn popper pooped, they were replaced with something new. When the marriage won't work and the pizzazz has pooped, why not the same fate? What impulse has put together, anything can put asunder.

The dangers here run deep. In relation to one another we learn our view of ourselves. If human life is considered trivial, then it's inevitable that sooner or later some groups will be considered disposable. The rise in the abortion rate today is exceeded only by the rise in the suicide rate for youth. Junk people are disposable people.

Here we may look to the church for an answer. But even churches have all too often displayed a blatant appetite for junk. In *A Long Obedience in the Same Direction* (subtitled "Discipleship in an Instant Society"), Eugene Peterson states,

> One aspect of world that I have been able to identify as harmful to Christians is the assumption that anything worthwhile can be acquired at once. We assume that if something can be done at all, it can be done quickly and efficiently. Our attention spans have been conditioned by

thirty-second commercials. Our sense of reality has been flattened by thirty-page abridgments. . . . In our kind of culture anything, even news about God, can be sold if it is packaged freshly: but when it loses its novelty, it goes on the garbage heap.[2]

Instant religion is junk religion. Junk religion replaces humble, compassionate service with "Smile, God Loves You" buttons. It replaces active, loving proclamation with "I'd Rather Be with Jesus" bumper stickers, "Fly the Rapture" Frisbees and other "Jesus junk." It produces people eager to wear the cross rather than bear the cross. "Give the people what they want"—and so we have drive-up and electronic churches: fast and anonymous. "If we become more like the world, the world will more likely listen to us," or so the argument goes. But we will probably also find that we no longer have anything worth saying.

How then do we argue against a mindset that has abandoned thoughtful arguments for media hype, prepackaged images and simplistic slogans? Do apologetics have any meaning in a society that gets its view of sexuality from "The Love Boat," its view of society from *People* magazine, and its view of the future from *The National Enquirer?*

We need to take to heart Paul's challenge to the Romans: "Do not conform any longer to the pattern of this world, but be transformed by the renewing of your mind." If we immerse our thoughts in nothing but the world around us, we can't hope to avoid adopting its attitudes. In both our churches and our personal devotions we must continually confront ourselves with God's character and his truth, and allow that truth to transform us. Only then can our lives be as light to a darkened world.

Quality, Elegance and Depth

The complexity of our day confronts us with a myriad of choices. But deciding can be such hard work! So we drift aimlessly from one passing diversion to another. God is eager to help us through our maze of choices, but all too often the most tempting response is, "No thank you, I'm just browsing." Living without depth or commitment, we can end up merely browsing through life. To affirm quality instead of embracing junk, we need to get beneath the surface. As we selectively invest ourselves in the important and valuable, our lives regain their elegance.

Junk may be elaborate or extravagant, but quality is elegant. This word is coming to mean merely "ritzy," but Webster still defines elegance as "tasteful richness of design, dignified gracefulness, or scientific precision, neatness and simplicity." In science an elegant theory fills all the needs of a situation with beautiful simplicity. Here is a goal for both our possessions and our activities.

Elegance in our lives demands discernment. We are called to set our minds only on that which is excellent and praiseworthy (Phil 4:8). We need to be asking ourselves in work, study and rest: Is this God's best for this moment?

This doesn't mean endless activity. When my life gets busy, I tend to fall into a state of perpetual motion where I feel every moment must somehow be "productive." We need our rest, times of deep relaxation and restoration, not just killing time with aimlessness. As Thoreau said, "As if we could kill time without injuring eternity." Assertiveness training is the topic of countless seminars, but assertiveness begins in learning to first say no to the internal demands of fear, pride and pointless habit so as to say yes to the one we call Lord. The price of this freedom is *internal* vigilance. Guided by God instead of goaded by the demands of the day, our lives regain their elegance.

We have the ability to be the best entertained, best informed people in history, but all too often we settle for hype and hoax, trivia and trash. Quality entertainment captures and portrays the essence of life; it stretches us—heart, mind and soul. Reading that informs, broadens and moves us is quality; a "fiction addiction" (John White's term) that devours our hours is junk. When television gives us a window on the world or provides us with thirty or sixty minutes of true entertainment, that is quality; when we turn on the tube blindly and watch an entire evening disappear, that is junk. Plays, movies and concerts that penetrate and celebrate life and lift us up are quality; those that delight in depicting depravity and drag us down are junk. Why pay for a guided tour of the gutter? Everything we see and do changes us; quality pulls us in the right direction.

Shallowness can also sap the genuine joy from our relationships. To acquire depth, our relationships must be built on trust strengthened over time. It's not possible to disclose ourselves to others all at once. We are each complex and unique, and to be intimate takes times and effort. It's a malaise of our society, the age of dial-a-sermon and love at first sight, that we want to instantly know a person. A true characteristic of openness is not to gush out with all that's inside us like a broken fire hydrant, but rather to seek to be completely honest and unpretentious in what we do reveal at the appropriate times.

Plastic replicas of friendship come cheaply and quickly; laying foundations in rock is hard work. But if people are as important to us as we claim, then it's worth laying deep foundations. For old things often lose their luster, but what can gladden us with its warm glow like an old friendship?

In our mobile society maintaining friendships takes real effort. A reason so many of us balk at letter writing is that this is a part of maintaining relationships that is work. I'm convinced that if the apostle Paul wrote letters the way I do, there would be nothing in the New Testament between Acts and Hebrews but a post card to the Corinthians: "Weather in Ephesus is fine, wish you were here." Instead, these letters are filled with thanksgiving, pleading, personal struggles, encouragement and exhortation. Separated by miles and sometimes years, Paul was still with his friends in spirit and in prayer, and he shared this at length.

It is true that we cannot be intimate with everyone we know, but we can be genuinely open with all and genuinely interested in all. In *Future Shock,* Alvin Toffler describes modern relationships: "We have created the disposable person: the Modular Man. Rather than entangling ourselves with the whole man, we plug into a module of his personality."[3]

God has given us the privilege and the calling of encountering whole people. Shallowness is content with the modular, disposable person, but beneath the surface is the unfolding of God's image, the unique, eternal person. Quality relationships grow from roots planted deeply.

Spiritual Therapy

Even our faith can be crippled by superficiality and thus needs to be transformed. Junk has one comforting quality, it never demands discipline. But without discipline we can never be disciples. We can't follow Jesus in Toyota's latest toy. We must learn to walk, day by day, in the same direction. When we trade the fellowship of believers for mere passing entertainment, changing churches like channels to suit our taste, we become spiritual invalids: overweight but undernourished, no longer able to stand before the Father nor follow the Son. Christ offers an answer, but it doesn't come on discount.

The Great Physician is not just a surgeon; he is also a spiritual therapist. After surgery comes the long mending process when we must work sore joints and aching muscles and bend reluctant tendons. This is work and it hurts. But we'll never see the fruit of surgery without it. The Physician's healing touch is first surgery—radical lifesaving surgery—but then comes the time we must work together: he, teaching and guiding—we, struggling, falling and trying again until we can walk, run and even soar like eagles. The question is, Will we settle for a Band-Aid or will we accept nothing less than total transformation?

Without this evidence of authentic faith, our cynical world can only scoff at our message. The unifying theme of the following chapters is authentic integrity, the deep simplicity of a pure heart, soul, mind and strength singly committed to our Lord. This is the faith that our junk-glutted society can recognize as radically different. Once they see it working out in our lives, they may consider dropping that armload of junk to accept this work of grace. When we've found God's best, we can discard the rest.

Jesus capsulizes this in a very short parable in Matthew 13:45-46: "The kingdom of heaven is like a merchant looking for fine pearls. When he found one of great value, he went away and sold everything he had and bought it." Everything in our lives should only be settings for displaying that pearl, and all aspects of our lives should be worthy of it.

THE ME GENERATION

LIVING IN AN AGE OF INDIVIDUALISM

3

There's a wall between us,
It's not made of stone.
The more we are together,
The more we are alone.
ANONYMOUS

THIS LITTLE POEM COULD EASILY BE THE LAMENT OF OUR AGE. Moviemakers obviously had fun in creating the story of Crocodile Dundee, an Australian from the remote outback who comes to New York City. He's convinced that any place with so many people living so closely together must be incredibly friendly. Needless to say, for him the Big Apple was full of surprises. Mr. Dundee discovers what Philip Slater described in *The Pursuit of Loneliness*:

It is easy to produce examples of the many ways in which Americans attempt to minimize, circumvent, or deny the interdependence upon which all human societies are based. We seek a private house, a private means of transportation, a private garden, a private laundry. . . . An enormous technology seems to have set itself the task of making it unnecessary for one human being ever to ask anything of another in the course of going about his daily business. Even within the family Americans are unique in their feeling that each member should have a separate room, and even a separate telephone, and car, when economically possible. We seek more and more privacy, and feel more and more alienated and lonely when we get it. . . . Our encounters with others tend increasingly to be competitive as a result of the search for privacy. We less and less often meet our fellow man to share and exchange, and more and more often encounter him as an impediment or a nuisance: making the highway crowded when we are rushing somewhere, cluttering and littering the beach or park or wood, pushing in front of us at the supermarket, taking the last parking place. . . . Because we have cut off so much communication with each other we keep bumping into each other, and thus a higher and higher percentage of our interpersonal contacts are abrasive.[1]

A quick glance at today's pop-psych best sellers shows that although we desire to build close, loving bonds, it appears we've forgotten how. Or maybe we are simply afraid. Or both.

Psychologist Erich Fromm maintains that the overwhelming fact of our existence is our aloneness. Perhaps more than any other people, this is true of Americans. Our heroes have always been loners. The American cowboy is many things, but above all he is alone. I grew up with Daniel Boone and Kit Carson: one man alone against the wilderness, his only friend his rifle. We're told it's lonely at the top, but Americans are experts at striving for the top. Family ties are often seen as shackles holding us down. And so we climb alone.

Much of the sixties' movement was a reaction against this view of personal success. Some escaped the establishment by entering communes, only to discover the futility of building a community centered on members "finding *themselves.*" The shift was made from seeking self-achievement to seeking self-actualization, but the focus was still self. As the counterculture waned, its deification of the individual became mainstream, and so laid the foundation for the self-actualization emphasis that helped usher in the Me Generation.

This thinking found its clearest expression from Gestalt psychotherapist Fritz Perls in words that, often with the last line omitted, found their way onto countless posters:

I'm not here to live up to your expectations,
Nor are you here to live up to mine.
I am I and you are you,
You do your thing and I'll do mine.
And if by chance we find each other, it's beautiful.
If not, it can't be helped.

Individual freedom remains our patron saint: you have a right to what you want as long as you don't stand in my way. Sings Billy Joel: "You can speak your mind, but not on my time."

It sounds like perfect freedom: to pursue our own happiness and only take care to stay out of one another's way. But what is the cost? Laments another song, "Freedom's just another word for nothing left to lose." Without bonds, instead of becoming free, we become merely aimless.

Writes Tom Howard:

Modern man is a bleak business. To our chagrin we discover that the declaration of autonomy has issued not in a race of free, masterly men, but rather in a race that can be described by its poets and dramatists only as bored, vexed, frantic, embittered, and sniffling.[2]

Berkeley sociologist Robert Bellah speaks of a "cancerous individualism" that threatens the survival of freedom itself as it undermines our society.[3]

A paradox of our times is that the generation with the most mediums of communication and interaction has become perhaps the most alone in history. Doctors are just beginning to fully discover how often this disease of aloneness is terminal. It kills our middle-aged and elderly with degenerative diseases and our youth by suicide, both in ever-increasing numbers. Stanford psychologist Philip Zimbardo writes,

> I know of no more potent killer than isolation. There is no more destructive influence on physical and mental health than the isolation of you from me and us from them. It has been shown to be a central agent in the etiology of depression, paranoia, schizophrenia, rape, suicide, mass murder, and a wide variety of disease states.[4]

Some die more subtly. You don't need to go to the latest horror movie to see the living dead; you probably live near a few. They don't get much notice hiding behind their doors and are usually avoided. Oh, they're still moving around, but there is no real life left in them; they're just too ornery to give people the satisfaction of their dying.

Conducting a study of isolated homeowners in Washington State gave me the opportunity to meet many fascinating but lonely people: the once eager entrepreneur who lost his wife and family along the way and now only had his two dogs for company (and all three of them snap at strangers); the not quite elderly couple who seemed terribly old and utterly cut off, venturing out only when they must; the manager who drove everyone to their limit and beyond by using every conversation as an exercise in intimidation until everyone was driven away; the interior decorator who designed places for everything except people, and now lived in a showpiece with no one for whom to show it. Somehow they never stopped to consider two important questions asked by Hillel in the Jewish Talmud: "If I am not for myself, who will be? If I am only for myself, what am I?"

But those on the fast track may not be any better off. With *Fortune* magazine in one hand and *Self* magazine in the other, they learn assertiveness, goal orientation, the art of selling oneself and of achieving a positive self-image—all with a concept of nothing but self. Is this the good life? It may seem so now, but I can't help asking with Jeremiah, "What will you do in the end?" (5:31). Is it the road to success? Maybe, but remember the warning of Proverbs: "There is a way that seems right to a man, but in the end it leads to death" (14:12).

One Lord, One Body

Not only his teaching but Jesus' entire life is a challenge to individualism. His unique relationship with his Father led not to mystic isolation, but to active involvement with people from all walks of life. His call to us as we encounter our neighbors is to "go and do likewise."

But individualism is even threatening to infiltrate our churches, some of which are becoming little more than isolated self-help centers. We hear cries to know God's will for *my* life, instead of the more biblical questions like, What is God's will for our hurting world? and What is his will for building his kingdom and how can I be a part of it? Yet these concerns sound foreign to Me Generation Christians. Christ is still the answer, but all the questions seem to have changed. Changed so much that popular Christian author and preacher Robert Schuller can proclaim the search for greater self-esteem as the new reformation.

The dilemma is illustrated by a Peanuts comic strip. Lucy, who has been in pursuit of inner peace, is back to threatening and bullying little brother Linus. Linus asks her, "But I thought you'd found inner peace." To which she responds, "Sure, I have inner peace, but I still have outer obnoxiousness." We can easily find ourselves in the same dilemma: pursuing spiritual gurus—including Christianity's latest—and continually seeking inner peace, but all the outside world sees is our outer obnoxiousness. Biblically, however, personal peace must always lead to interpersonal peace. The gospel offers peace, but it also calls us to be peacemakers.

A healthy concept of who we are is important, but it must begin in a healthy concept of who God is. It's not as important *who* we are as *whose* we are. Scripture offers us many insights about who we are, but above all the New Testament teaches us that we are members of the body of Christ. Our essential identity is not an individual identity but a corporate one. I'm a member of something that goes far beyond my own little world. This isn't so strange a concept in Eastern cultures where people are often reluctant to respond with personal decisions for the gospel, since anything so important must be a community or family decision. In the West, however, we must be continually reminded that we are not an ensemble of individuals who are trying to learn to be nice to one another; we are grafted in, baptized into *one* body.

Paul never seemed to tire of emphasizing this fact: "The body is a unit, though it is made up of many parts; and though all its parts are many, they form one body" (1 Cor 12:12). "In Christ we who are many form one body, and each member belongs to all the others" (Rom 12:5). "From him the whole body, joined and held together by every supporting ligament, grows and builds itself up in love, as each part does its work" (Eph 4:16). "Each of you must put off falsehood and speak truthfully to his neighbor, for we are all members of one body" (Eph 4:25). "Submit to one another out of reverence for Christ" (Eph 5:21). "Let the peace of Christ rule in your hearts, since as members of one body you were called to peace" (Col 3:15).

Too Close for Comfort

"One body," "belong to one another," "submit to one another"—what strange phrases in our society! Do they have anything at all in common with our modern churches? Do we honestly desire them to? At times it's exciting to read the accounts of the early disciples' sharing in Acts: "They devoted themselves to the apostles' teaching and to the fellowship, to the breaking of bread and to prayer. . . . Selling their possessions and goods, they gave to anyone as he had need. . . . They broke bread in their homes and ate together with glad and sincere hearts" (2:42, 45-46). "All the believers were one in heart and mind. No one claimed that any of his possessions was his own, but they shared everything they had" (4:32). But at other times we might prefer to echo the sentiments of a poet, who perhaps for obvious reasons chose to remain anonymous:

Oh to dwell there above
With the saints that we love,
That will be such glory.

But to dwell here below
With the saints that we know,
That's another story!

Living our lives as members of one body can be uncomfortable
and awkward at times; it can also be disturbing and even
frightening. But it's not as frightening as the alternative. One
thing comes out again and again in therapy. Fears and anx-
ieties breed loneliness and then grow in that lonely void. Not
only don't we share our inner selves with others, we don't even
share them with ourselves. We end up burying the hurts, and
eventually they fester. Once we share ourselves with one another and enjoy acceptance, then we are on the way to being
healed.

We are called to be lovingly accountable to one another:
making decisions together, seeking advice and counsel, being
open to encouragement and admonishment, sharing our lives,
holding up the standards of the penetrating light of the Word
to one another. This should not be a threat, but a comfort. The
only truly peaceful sense of privacy lies in having nothing to
hide.

We all have an interest in people and their affairs. Cut off
from the deeper side of one another, our society indulges this
interest by watching "Dallas," reading scandal sheets and gos-
siping about rumors. But our interest in others was meant to
inspire sincere counsel and compassion, not spicy conversation. This means moving from detached observation to true
involvement.

Chuck Swindoll lists three ingredients of meaningful involvement: vulnerability, spontaneity and accountability.[5] Being vulnerable means beginning to express what's inside—first

to our spouse or a close friend, and then gradually to others. This can be awkward and frightening since we have been taught by society that appearances and first impressions matter most. The prized look is the self-confident, wry strength of the *Gentleman's Quarterly* man, or the radiant total woman of *Glamour*. Being vulnerable goes directly against this value since it entails the risk of entrusting ourselves to another.

Christians have not always promoted vulnerability either. In many circles we're led to believe that brokenness is something that happens only before conversion; after that we always have "victory, victory, victory in Jesus." Admitting weakness is seen as an admission of defeat or a lack of faith.

Like so many, I find it far easier to minister than be ministered to. For me, sharing ideas has come freely; sharing feelings has always seemed awkward and clumsy. When I did try to open up more, sometimes I found it almost impossible— not because I lacked the desire, but because I lacked the vocabulary. Feelings do not go readily into words without practice. Fortunately, I've had friends and a wife who could model vulnerable honesty and who weren't content to remain "on the outside." I'm learning what we all must realize: the only true security lies in honest vulnerability.

Second, we need to be spontaneous in showing affection. In *The Friendship Factor*, Alan Loy McGinnis gives this rule for deepening relationships: "Dare to talk about your affection." He goes on to say this:

For fear of seeming sentimental, many of us hold back expressions of warmth and thereby miss out on rich and profound friendships. We say "thanks" when we mean "God bless you," and "so long" when we mean "I'll miss you a lot." G. K. Chesterton once said that the meanest fear is the fear of sentimentality. I would add immeasurably to the amount of love abroad if we would be freer in declaring our affection.[6]

Call people up; seek them out; offer spontaneous encouragement. We shouldn't wait until we're saying final good-by's to tell people how much we care about them. Many are dying (in some cases literally) for a single kind and caring word; we can't afford to be stingy with our affection.

Finally, we need to be accountable to each other. Many of us have a cynical view of advice (due, no doubt, to its frequent abuse), but how different was the view of the ancients. Proverbs resounds with refrains like this one: "The way of a fool seems right to him, but a wise man listens to advice" (12:15). I remember the lonely responsibility of making a major career choice while in rural Washington, far from the counsel of family and friends, and how frightening this "freedom" can be. I've made too many stupid, scary choices because I made them alone (after all, others "just wouldn't understand").

Wisdom may come to a sage on a mountaintop, but most often it comes in caring communities. In some ways I'm as stubborn as ever, but how refreshing it has been to say, "I know I need to make the final choice, but what do you think?" What a nice compliment to pay someone, admitting we value his or her insights. It requires vulnerability to admit we're unsure and to expose our fragmentary and incomplete thoughts and plans to another's scrutiny, but "Wisdom lies in much counsel." In this age that worships independence, we need to relearn the joy of healthy, balanced interdependence.

A Family of Families
Mistaking socializing for hearty fellowship is a common error

in our churches. Socializing is pleasant, but it is not the solution to our deepest needs. Without open, self-giving love the church can become just another organization. Our age of the individual is also the age of the organization man, Homo Corporatus, where every activity (including art and marriage) is conducted by contract. Swindoll says, "We are independent cogs in complex corporate structures."[7] Don't make the error of lonely executives and socialites—organization is not community. Our churches *have* and need organization, but they are called to *be* caring communities. Organization without community is for ants, not people.

The church must move from existing as an organization of associates to becoming a family of families. J. C. Wynn describes this process:

> The church must also renew its concept of "the family of God" as a metaphor for the church itself. Charles Stewart (1979) has argued for the contemporary congregation to become a virtual extended family, gathering in the different generations of the parish to become what they are meant to be: the household of God.
>
> The church as an extended family can reach out to the lonely, support the weak, help the helpless, and love the unlovable. That's what families, when they are at their best, do for their members.[8]

Right after college, when I was single and moving frequently, I remember how special it was to find a rare church whose members did not just smile at me on Sunday morning, but welcomed me into an extended family. Some offered meals; some introduced me to other church members and to the community; one offered me a place to stay for a week while I was apartment hunting; one showed me how I could, in

45

return, serve members valuably. This ministry is especially vital when so many today are without full families. Even couples may be lonely twosomes when work and mobility have cut them off from family ties. Members need more than the friendship of those of similar age and interests; they also need the family-wide fellowship of the whole church body.

We need to ask ourselves in what ways we can begin to foster this sense of family in our own church. In a larger church this level of caring will involve shaping smaller groups (never to become isolated from the whole, however). If the church's groups are segregated by age, encourage intergenerational interaction. Brainstorm together on ways to serve one another and the church as a whole. Joan Wulff describes this process in her own small group:

> The small group I'm in is creating community informally. A guy-friend picks me up at the airport. A girlfriend changes the oil in my car. A couple lends me warm coats, gloves and hats when my California family members come to Chicago in February. I baby-sit so others can have a night out; I prepare a meal for someone who is sick. Plumbing has been fixed, cars lent, beds offered by people to others in the group. And we all pray for each other.[9]

This concern isn't an appendix to the gospel but is at its very center: "[Christ] died for all, that those who live should no longer live for themselves" (2 Cor 5:15). It is also at the center of our presentation of the gospel. Christ prayed that we might be one as he and the Father are one *so that the world may believe* the Father sent him (Jn 17:22-23). Only as we build this biblical form of fellowship can we fulfill Paul's directive: "Do everything without complaining or arguing, so that you may be blameless and pure . . . as you hold out the word of life" (Phil

2:14-16). Ours is not to be a closed community, holding back in isolation, but a contagious community, holding out an invitation. True community is born out of mission.

Active Love

Love is an active verb. It is constantly reaching out, always initiating as it responds to God, the great initiator. Fellowship within the church is not intended to become so comfortable that it becomes exclusive, but it is to be constantly overflowing into our world. The opposite of love isn't hate—it's indifference.

One way to actively love is to listen. Good listening is more than just keeping our mouths shut, and it's more than just waiting our turn to talk. Listening with love is taking an active interest in other people's lives and expressing that care. We need to become a part of someone's world—in its fascination, joy, pain and confusion—and express our empathy in our posture, expression and response. Don't let your thoughts drift away but keep them focused. Be aware of eye contact. Apparent indifference makes people feel insignificant. Listening is getting out of ourselves long enough to actively share in someone's life.

We must also learn to see people lovingly. They say that love is blind. Yet godly love doesn't use blindfolds but binoculars. It sees not only what the person is like, but also all what this person is becoming. It sees not only the present person but also the potential person. We need to take the time to take a second look, to re-examine our attitudes toward the people in our life. Love is realistic, but it enables us to see the flower in the cactus, the butterfly in the worm. Love transforms not only how we listen but also how we see.

Finally, we must learn to lovingly act. The world knows about loving actions, but these are usually based on loving feelings. In the kingdom the actions come first, then the feelings follow. When we love the unlovable, they begin to change. They begin to conform, not to our expectations, but to our love. They slowly gain lovability and love of their own. It works. It's the process God began in us.

We are to be prepared to express God's love "in season and out of season," to correct and encourage with great patience (see 2 Tim 4:2). I remember traveling alone cross-country, eager for the warm fellowship of friends at Bear Trap Ranch in Colorado. But because of a bus strike, I ended up in a crowded bus station in Denver, bus-lagged and dog-tired, sitting in the middle of three wandering winos. One, a man in his late twenties with surprising insights behind his slurred speech, wanted to talk; he was tired of the road and wanted a way out. And so we talked (and all the while I wondered when I could get away). My escape involved a short hitchhike with a long-winded hot-air balloonist struggling with a self-defeating lifestyle. Then came another late-night layover at a tiny bus station with a lonely janitor who was fighting a seemingly dead-end life. Throughout these conversations I found myself looking ahead to seeing my friends and enjoying the conversations I had planned. But in the process I finally realized I was avoiding people who desperately needed a listening ear and sincere encouragement. Godly love sets down no preconditions; it shows itself true in all seasons.

These expressions of active love are not limited to strangers. In fact, most of our love will be expressed to those who already surround us—parents, grandparents, friends, neighbors, co-workers. This love can be costly. People complicate things.

Going it alone is often easier, but its rarely better. Eliminating people from our lives rarely, in the end, makes things truly simpler, just starker. People complicate our lives, but people also enrich our lives—especially those who are not like us. We can rejoice over differences because they are a reflection of God's creativity. By surrounding ourselves with children, the elderly, foreign and distinctively ethnic people, people of widely different vocations and educational levels, we can learn from all and enjoy all; laughter comes in groups.

Perls offered the best advice he had, but as Christians we must revise his words:

I'm not here to live up to your expectations,
Nor are you here to live up to mine.
Together we seek to follow our one Master,
And so we walk side by side.
I am I and you are you,
But we are Christ's.
We do the things he commands;
We find ourselves in him.
And in so doing we find one another,
And it is beautiful.

Jesus said he gave us the command to love one another as he loved us, "that your joy may be full" (Jn 15:11). Our lives are full when we share fully in the lives of others. We must never try to live people's lives for them, but we are called to live our lives with them. Then the world will look at us the way the Roman world looked at the early Christian community in astonishment and said, "See how these Christians love one another!" Welcome to the We Generation!

THE
CLUTTERED
GENERATION

LIVING IN AN AGE OF MATERIALISM

4

*He who dies with
the most toys wins.*
BUMPER STICKER

TO SPEAK OF MATERIALISM WHEN DISCUSSING OUR SOCIETY HAS become almost a cliché. Many of us are tired of hearing of the dangers of wealth and affluence while trying to make ends meet or worrying about the possibility of losing our jobs. But the issue is not wealth; the world has always had its rich. Rather it is that in the Junk Generation even the poorer classes have more "stuff" at their disposal than most of history's wealthy. We don't need to be rich to be affected by our materialistic society. From the ghettos to the penthouse suites, most people find themselves living cluttered lives in cluttered worlds. Our lives have become the by-products of mass production. As a group we are no longer citizens, countrymen or comrades; we are merely lumped together as "consumers." The credo of modern society's identity could well be, "I consume; therefore I am."

Name Dropping

From our cradles to our crypts the world cajoles us to acquire. The ancient Hebrews wrote the Law on their gates and doorposts and wore it on their hems and foreheads. We do the same, but ours is the law of supply and demand. Our clocks, notepads, utensils and posters all carry the logos of the latest "in" products. Our expensive clothes parade their designers, and our T-shirts proclaim either our favorite beer or our favorite sports equipment. Our phylacteries are headbands printed with our patron products. Our athletes aren't awarded laurels; they're awarded commercial contracts to wear conspicuous brand-name labels. Why shouldn't our entertainment be filled with commercials when our lives are filled with them? Sparta was the land of the soldier; Phoenicia the land of the sailor; America is the land of the salesperson.

Why is this marketing onslaught so successful? Clearly it is only human to desire comforts, but we seem to spend more time and effort obtaining and maintaining our stuff than it ever saves us. The advertisers succeed because they have learned to appeal to two things even more foundational than our desire for comfort: our pride and our fear.

Possession offers us a strange sense of vicarious pride. We all desire to be acclaimed, to be the best, to be inherently competent, to be unique and special. The path to these achievements, however, is invariably long and difficult. What the advertisers offer us is a short cut—it's easier to buy than to become, to consume than to create. We can then quickly have something admirable. After all, don't clothes make the man? We hope so. The motto for today is "You are what you wear." Or smoke. Or drive.

Media hype plays on our immaturity. Of course no truly great lover would really need the latest cigarette, cologne or aftershave; these would be secondary, trivial concerns. Still this advertising is perfectly suited to the Junk Generation: to be a new person is easy; all you need is a new brand of toothpaste. The result of this possessive pursuit of pride is that we find ourselves in a ludicrous trap where "we buy things we do not want to impress people we do not like."[1]

Second, hype plays not only on immaturity, but also on insecurity:

How many times must a guy spray with Ban
    Before he doesn't offend?
And how many times must he gargle each day
    Before he can talk to a friend?
How many tubes of shampoo must he buy
    Before his dandruff will end?
The sponsors, my friend, will sell you all they can.
    The sponsors will sell you all they can.[2]

The classic commercials today portray what people are thinking behind our backs: "Too bad about that dandruff," or "Oh, what breath!" This is the ultimate manipulation—even if you have no apparent need for the product, who knows what people are thinking behind your back? We're afraid and the advertisers know it. Writes Ron Sider:

A bank in Washington, D.C. recently advertised for new savings accounts with the question, "Who's gonna love you when you're old and grey?" Our savings bank sponsors a particularly enticing ad, "Put a little love away. Everybody needs a penny for a rainy day. Put a little love away." Those words are unbiblical, heretical, demonic. They teach the Big Lie of our secular, materialistic society. But the words and music are so seductive that they dance through my head hundreds of times.

He concludes by quoting a designer speaking about his exceedingly expensive jewelry: "A nice piece of jewelry you can relate to is like having a friend who's always there."[3] Security once meant family, friends and faith; now it means ownership. "I've got an IRA; I'll be OK."

A Prisoner of Desire

What's wrong with a little planning? Nothing—until it becomes a substitute for faith. What's wrong with consumerism? Nothing—until it begins to consume us. Our security can become our prison, a trap of our own making. Consumerism traps us in the very anxiety we sought to escape. Dietrich Bonhoeffer comments on Matthew 6:25-34,

Be not anxious! Earthly possessions dazzle our eyes and delude us into thinking that they can provide security and freedom from anxiety. Yet all the time they are the very source of anxiety. If our hearts are set on them, our reward is an anxiety whose burden is intolerable. Anxiety creates its own treasures and they in turn beget further care. When we seek for security in possessions we are trying to drive out care with care, and the net result is the precise opposite of our anticipations. The fetters which bind us to our possessions prove to be cares themselves.[4]

As Kahlil Gibran put so simply in *The Prophet:* "And what is fear of need but need itself? Is not dread of thirst when your well is full the thirst that is unquenchable?"[5]

Not only do we become trapped in a vicious cycle of anxiety, but we also become trapped in a cycle of avarice. This is the "middle-class trap" that snares so many idealistic college students. After graduation a job brings increasing responsibility. This in turn pressures these new professionals into greater acquisitions to better "play the part." These acquisitions only add to the responsibility. Next they feel they need a new car to go with the new job, but now the expense of that better car demands a still better job, even if it's unsatisfying. Thus their possessions, rather than becoming their servants, have become their masters. The range of what they consider necessary continues to grow, and now freedom always seems to lie behind one more installment payment. Their mortgage bankers meet them at the door with a smile and a greeting, "Welcome to the middle class."

This is a trend which can only get worse. Writes Boorstin: "We will be misled if we think that technology will be directed primarily to satisfying 'demands' or 'needs' or to solving 'problems.' . . . Technology is a way of multiplying the unnecessary."[6] Mark Twain summed it up best: "Civilization is a limitless multiplication of unnecessary necessities."

Another danger of materialism is that it can consume our faith as it insulates us. Our ancestors walked out in the elements and were continually reminded of their frailty and dependence on God. But when light and heat come with the turn of a switch, we can imagine ourselves to be sovereigns. We can reign so long as we can pay our utility bills. Materialism dulls our sense of delight and our sense of need and so leads to the Bored Generation.

The Cluttered Generation is the complacent generation. Our

great danger is security in complacency. We often can say with the song, "It's all very nice, just not very good." We trade God's best for something less, but with our wealth we at least get something that's comfortable. But when the ultimate choice is heaven or hell, it's wise not to settle for second best.

We are also consumed as materialism isolates us. The man or woman walking to the neighborhood market can't help but meet and greet neighbors. Sealed in the family car, however, the only companion is the (all too often) droning drivel of the car radio. Douglas Webster describes this:

We are first and foremost consumers. This is no new fact. It can be argued that there is very little difference between the man who fights for survival and the man who lives for pleasure. Essentially they are both materialists. But what is especially characteristic of modern man's affluence is that he has chosen things over people. No longer do we envision security and happiness primarily in terms of human relationships and our relationship to God. People become functionaries only as valuable as the dollar value of the task they perform. Affluence has led us to a very real sense of isolation. We are imprisoned by things, related to one another through things, brought together on account of things, and separated because of things.[7]

This is the tragedy of affluence. Through the ages the wealthy and powerful have often viewed people in terms of economic value and faced the resulting isolation, but now this option is open to all of us. The consumers have become the consumed.

To Have or to Be

What does this creeping clutter mean for us as Christians? The church has always been somewhat schizophrenic in its approach to material wealth. The Middle Ages gave us both gilded basilicas and ascetic monks. The debate continues today in discussions of building projects versus mission activities. The church offers living water to our world, but should it foremost be a beautiful oasis, saying, "Come and drink," or Jacob's well, sending out rescue parties with dented canteens and the message, "Go out and serve"?

Robert Schuller argues his case for the oasis model in defending his Crystal Cathedral:

> We are trying to make a big, beautiful impression upon the affluent, nonreligious American who is riding by on this busy freeway. . . . But suppose we had given this money to feed the poor? What would we have today? We would still have hungry poor people and God would not have this tremendous base of operations which he is using to inspire people.[8]

But are we called to be inspired or transformed? It is true that as we look more and more like the world, the world is more likely to listen to us, but we may well find that we no longer have anything worth saying. The greatest hurdle we face in presenting the gospel in the Western world is not ignorance but cynicism; the great unmet need is not so much for people to hear the gospel but to see the gospel. To see it in us. Cut crystal is a poor substitute for shining stars. Douglas Webster writes, "The time is now for whole churches to reassess their priorities and to implement voluntary programs of living and giving which are sacrificial instead of superficial."[9]

Timothy faced similar problems amidst the wealth and poverty of the urban world of first-century Ephesus. Paul's reminder to him can be a reminder to us all:

> Godliness with contentment is great gain. For we brought

nothing into the world, and we can take nothing out of it. But if we have food and clothing, we will be content with that. People who want to get rich fall into temptation and a trap and into many foolish and harmful desires that plunge men into ruin and destruction. For the love of money is a root of all kinds of evil. Some people, eager for money, have wandered from the faith and pierced themselves with many griefs. (1 Tim 6:6-10)

Paul's answer to worldly materialism is not stark asceticism—the mere giving up of things. In fact, Paul's solution doesn't deal with things at all: "But you, man of God, flee from all this, and pursue righteousness, godliness, faith, love, endurance and gentleness" (1 Tim 6:11). Paul's solution involves character. This is the real issue which confronts us. Erich Fromm describes our choice in the title of one of his books, *To Have or to Be?* Remember the appeal of hype to our pride and fear. Insecure of who we are we turn to things. We hide from our insignificance behind great, imposing piles of clutter.

Jesus describes this attitude in his parable of the rich fool, the man who felt secure because his barns were full—until his soul was required of him. "This is how it will be," Jesus said, "with anyone who stores up things for himself but is not rich toward God" (Lk 12:21). The parable strikingly illustrates his warning: "Be on your guard against all kinds of greed; a man's life does not consist in the abundance of his possessions" (Lk 12:15).

Our material society hasn't changed one essential fact: you never see hearses pulling U-Hauls. You can take nothing with you but what you have become.

Peter warns women against outward adornment in favor of inward beauty, and the admonition applies to all of us. We are not to strike the world with the shine of our new cars but with the shine of eyes filled with the joy of Jesus; not with the size of our houses but with the size of hearts filled with his love. When we are whole, we need no longer attempt to fill our inadequacies with things. Authenticity invariably shows itself in simplicity.

Breaking Free

To be authentic witnesses, our break with materialism must be complete—sacrificial not superficial. We can no longer simply ask, "Am I living beyond *my* means?"—that is the question of the Me Generation. Rather, we must look at the needs of our world and the needs of our church and ask, "Am I living beyond *our* means?"

Jesus didn't allow us the option of comfortable compromise: "No one can serve two masters. Either he will hate the one and love the other, or he will be devoted to the one and despise the other. You cannot serve both God and Money" (Mt 6:24). The reason is a simple one: "For where your treasure is, there your heart will be also" (Mt 6:21)—and your mind and your strength and even your very soul. This is the danger of materialism: it is a subtle obsession. It commands our allegiance and cripples our faith.

First, materialism commands our allegiance. Whatever is motivating us at any given moment is lord of that moment. Most of us claim that material goods are low on our list of priorities, and yet look at how much of our time and effort is consumed by them. Dietrich Bonhoeffer wrote about our divided loyalties:

Earthly goods are given to be used, not to be collected. In the wilderness God gave Israel the manna every day, and they had no need to worry about food and drink. Indeed, if they kept any of the manna over until the next day, it went bad. In the same way, the disciple must receive his portion from God every day. If he stores it up as a permanent possession, he spoils not only the gift, but himself as well, for he sets his heart on his accumulated wealth, and makes it a barrier between himself and God. Where our treasure is, there is our trust, our security, our consolation and our God. Hoarding is idolatry.[10]

Second, materialism cripples our faith. The pursuit of God is hard enough without us laying hurdles on our path or weights on our backs. Judy Peace tells the story of a young African man who was utterly unable to believe there could be such a thing as an atheist. Finally, he responded, "I know you wouldn't lie to me, so there must be these people who don't believe in God; but all I can say is that they must be very rich." She had to agree. Perhaps not rich by our standards, but sufficiently materialistic to be so busy collecting and polishing trinkets that they missed the "pearl of great price."

Our problem is not so much that our homes are cluttered as it is that our hearts are cluttered. Richard Foster comments, If what we have we receive as a gift, and if what we have is to be cared for by God, and if what we have is available to others, then we will possess freedom from anxiety. This is the inward reality of simplicity. However, if what we have we believe we have gotten, and if what we have we believe we must hold onto, and if what we have is not available to others, then we will live in anxiety. Such persons will never know simplicity regardless of the outward contortions they may put themselves through in order to live "the simple life."[11]

A person may be free with a barn full of stuff or enslaved to the belongings of a small apartment. And yet attitude always shows itself in action.

Clearing Out the Clutter

To return our allegiance to our Lord and to revive our faith we must build on what God has freely given us—our heart, our mind and our strength. His concern is not what we have but what we have become. A life of authentic simplicity—focused on being rather than having—will be marked by freedom, contentment, sharing, creativity, stewardship and generosity.

Freedom. George MacDonald wrote, "To have what we want is riches; to do without is power." The title of a book by Richard Foster also says a great deal, *The Freedom of Simplicity.* Simplicity, cheerfully doing without, is freedom. And it is true power.

Our entire society is geared to pressuring us into acquiring more now: one-time offers, buy-now/pay-later plans, ten-day trial offers, one-day-only coupons and so on. Countering this pressure takes godly self-control. We must slow down enough to evaluate our actions: what would I do if the item simply weren't available? Can I borrow, share, create, make do or improvise? Is it necessary? Is it truly beneficial? Never rush to buy. Since this wooing plays on our subconscious, we need to make patient, prayerful, conscious decisions. See if God will provide without our rushing to the shopping mall. We can discuss our needs with family and friends; they may have suggestions, tips, or perhaps something to loan or sell inexpensively. If we begin to think creatively, we will find many alternatives to the acquisition mania our society instills in us.

When Susan and I were married, we acquired our double

bed from her teen-age brother for five dollars and a box of Twinkies (and he got the better end of the deal!). But that bed held us until we found an ideal French provincial garage-sale special. Some touch-up work was all that was needed to give us an attractive, quality bedroom set. Most newlyweds have similar stories of making do, but how easy it is to forget the fun and freedom of making do once steady paychecks begin, and "settledness" settles in.

The purpose of all this is freedom. We need to learn to laugh at manipulative advertising and become connoisseurs, choosing the best and ignoring the rest. By living deliberately, we can live intelligently and have only one Lord.

Contentment. "Godliness with contentment is great gain" (1 Tim 6:6). The danger of overabundance is that it can satiate and deaden us to the wonder of life. We need to enjoy the small stuff. As I sit in our little apartment, I'm enjoying the painting on the wall (an original hand-me-down from Susan's grandmother), Susan's violets (they finally bloomed like they show in the pictures), our pump organ (on loan as long as our long-suffering neighbors don't complain), the snow settling into the evergreens while I'm warm inside. We enjoy walks and looking over our big back yard (a college campus). What are you enjoying these days?

Sharing. Private ownership is the proud hallmark of America. Controlled, it is the foundation of free enterprise; uncontrolled, it becomes an enslaving enterprise. We often own things not just to have access to them, but because we believe possession gives us control. This is the great irony: our desire to manipulate our world is the very desire that allows us to be manipulated by the world.

For all we complain (sometimes rightfully) of public lands

and buildings, they're a great resource. I remember the frustration of driving the coast of southern Maine and being unable to get near the ocean because of private land and "No Trespassing" signs. How different it was to drive the southern Oregon coast and stop at will at countless public parks and beaches. Places vary in the amount of public facilities they offer, but almost anywhere offers facilities—parks, forests, wildlife refuges and beaches—which we commonly ignore. Public libraries, civic centers and museums are other examples of institutional *sharing*.

Shouting "Mine! Mine!" is for three-year-olds. We need to take a fresh look at the first disciples who "had all things in common." A friend of ours shares a snow blower with both of his next-door neighbors. This also allows them to help each other out by doing a neighbor's driveway as well as their own when they have the time.

Jesus gives the disciples a fascinating promise after they've watched him interact with a man trapped by his riches. He says to them, "I tell you the truth . . . no one who has left home or brothers or sisters or mother or father or children or fields for me and the gospel will fail to receive a hundred times as much in this present age" (Mk 10:29-30). What does he mean by "in this present age"? Certainly the disciples never became rich. But they did become part of a sharing church (note that they gain brothers and sisters as well as homes and fields). It is no coincidence that the Me Generation is also the Cluttered Generation. Individualism and materialism are invariably twins. When we have the caring fellowship of people we can trust, we no longer need to seek security in things.

Simple hospitality is a way of sharing our homes and ourselves. Donald Bubna was frustrated at the way his congregation openly accepted his preaching on hospitality but then failed to practice it. Finally, a church questionnaire showed that the primary reason for their reluctance was the feeling that "our home furnishings are too modest or inadequate." Other surveys in other churches showed the same thing: fear and insecurity were at work as people expected others to judge them on what they owned. His task was to convey a truer understanding of Christian hospitality, one which says, "We don't have much furniture, but we'd like to have you come. We don't have elegant food, but we can whip up some pancakes. We'd like you to see us the way we are, so come as you are. We'll get to know you better."[12]

Churches can do much to promote sharing. They can have a bulletin board of items or services to share, loan or give away or a community closet of no longer needed items. Church grounds or a little used portion of a member's large yard can become the congregation's community garden. Job networks can be set up where church youth can work for church business people. The first chapters of Acts does not have to be limited to the first century. The patterns may differ, but the results will be the same.

Creativity. "The problem with living simply is that it gets so complicated!" Do you sometimes feel that way? Swimming against the tide is never easy. The solution is to not try to change everything at once. We were snared by consumerism one strand at a time; to become free we need to break one strand at a time. To do this we must be creative.

Have you ever seen a Japanese home? Every inch is used several times over: beds roll up; tables fold down; walls shift in and out. Truly "necessity is the mother of invention" in their case, but creativity can be fun. Instead of seeking larger quarters, we can maximize the use of our space: bunk beds for children, roll-out drawers under the bed, shelves for walls and closets, storage bins for attics, basements and crawl spaces. Ingenuity is supposed to be the American way; have fun with it.

Do you have a yard? Try growing vegetables instead of uninterrupted grass. If not, try window-box and indoor gardening. When my grandparents moved from their farm into town, they brought as much of the farm as they could to that little city lot. It was amazing to see what they could grow in their own back yard! Remember, gardening is the world's oldest profession (Gen 2).

Transportation is another area where we can be creative. By using our legs or a bike we can burn carbohydrates instead of hydrocarbons. Using public transportation not only conserves energy, it may preserve our sanity by letting someone else worry about rush-hour traffic. An alternative is to share morning devotions with car-pooling friends on the way to work.

Being creative in our interactions with children is especially rewarding. We can design projects using "left over" items or simply go exploring. By finding activities that feed their imagination and not their greed, we develop children that are inquisitive instead of acquisitive.

Creativity often gives us a third option when we are facing a "to buy or not to buy" situation: Do we need to invest in something new or to invest ourselves in creatively using the old? Do we need to invest in more effort-saving equipment, or to invest ourselves in healthy activity? Do we need to invest in new clothes and furniture or to invest ourselves in learning mending, refinishing and rearranging?

Conformity to clutter weighs us down and limits our lives.

Creativity, on the other hand, is active and freeing. It takes time and commitment, but it is also fun and rewarding—like most things in life that are worthwhile.

Stewardship. Stewardship is an old idea, but one often foreign to our way of thinking. It simply means that what we have is not our possession, but something entrusted to our care. How much of our money does God want? All of it, and everything else we have. All of our buying, spending and acquiring must be done with full regard for our responsibility to the total community and to the Giver of all good gifts.

This demands moment-by-moment discipleship. The "small" temptations like lust and drunkenness we only have to deal with occasionally, and for some of us, not at all. Avarice, on the other hand, in a society where absolutely everything is on sale, is a constant threat. This shouldn't be a debilitating weight, but an exciting challenge. Every intelligent choice is an opportunity to grow and become more free of clutter.

Stewardship has implications for the big "haves" of our lives and the way we use them. I hear Christians beamingly say of their possessions, "Oh yes, this is God's house," or, "Yes, God gave us this wonderful new car, and it's dedicated to him." Do those words have any reality behind them? One can find out quickly by asking to use that big car to transport a junior-high church club, or by asking to put up a needy stranger in that big house. If we truly have an attitude of stewardship, then it will be evident in the lack of anxiety we have for our possessions, and the naturalness of our giving.

Stewardship also has implications for the small "haves" of our lives and the way we acquire them. Practicality replaces pride as the primary motivation for purchases. Lasting quality replaces passing fads as our criteria for purchases. Susan has an Air Force parka that she's worn through ten Minnesota winters. That's value. I have a suede leather jacket that I bought on impulse when it seemed like a good buy. That jacket soon developed more cracks in it than the San Andreas Fault. That's junk. Stewardship doesn't mean always buying the cheapest; it means only buying when necessary and then doing so on the basis of value, not hype. It is quality over junk.

Generosity. One word separates simple living from miserly living—*generosity.* Saving can become as much of an obsession as spending; what begins in prudence ends in slavery. To insure that we don't trade one obsession for another, we must learn the joy of generosity. The joy of generosity comes when we give not out of grudging duty but out of cheerful gratitude. "God loves a cheerful giver" (2 Cor 9:7). "Cheerful" here is from the Greek word *hilaros,* which means "cheerful, glad, light, joyful," with perhaps "kind and gracious." It's the root for our word *hilarious.*

What a privilege God has given us to be givers as he is! With this in mind, our stern responsibility should become gracious hilarity. We give because it is our nature, as God gives because it is his nature: "They give as in yonder valley the myrtle breathes its fragrance into space. Through the hands of such as these God speaks."[13]

I am not suggesting that we give with reckless stupidity. Sadly, there is probably more hype behind many "charities" than behind most commercial products. This hype succeeds because we give out of guilt manipulation rather than out of stewardship. When we give, we invest ourselves, and so here as with all else we must be asking, "What is God's best? Where are the needs the greatest and the resources the least? Has this group proven themselves faithful stewards?" This demands understanding, an understanding that only comes from investing ourselves in the needs of our world. We are both to give deliberately and joyously.

How do we make giving this natural? Simply through giving. Susan amazes me by beginning to put together Christmas gifts sometimes in May. This is not because she's so efficient, but because she delights in giving and is constantly thinking of "just what so and so needs." Christmas is only merry once we learn to be merry givers. But we are not limited to giving things. We can also give of our home through hospitality or encouragement through unexpected notes and visits.

We also need to lay a foundation beneath this spontaneous and incidental giving by establishing a plan for organized giving: giving a percentage of our income to the church and other appropriate organizations. The ten-per-cent tithe of the Old Testament Law may provide a good place to begin. Whatever the level, it is our pledge before God. No one would invest haphazardly in earthly securities, how much more should our investment in the kingdom of God be a carefully planned commitment.

At the same time we learn to be generous givers, we must be careful not to develop a benevolence complex. We must allow others the joy of giving to us lest we become stingy receivers. God wants us to gratefully receive all that he offers us. "Freely you have *received*, freely give" (Mt 10:8). It is because of the one that we can do the other. This is the mystery of the economics of the kingdom that neither the capitalists nor the Marxists will ever understand: "One man gives freely, yet gains even more; another withholds unduly, but comes to poverty. A generous man will prosper; he who refreshes others will himself be refreshed" (Prov 11:24-25).

The Abundant Life

"I desired all things that I might enjoy life; God gave me life that I might enjoy all things." It's always been true. It's the secret of the kingdom, and we shouldn't keep it a secret any longer.

Spontaneous giving breaks down barriers. A life free from mindless materialism will show the Cluttered Generation the path to freedom as surely as stars on a dark night. We need only cease clinging to our clutter. With one hand holding on tight to what we've got, and one hand grasping for more, we've nothing left with which to be reaching out. This is the tragedy of the church. Jerome wrote of the early church in its new-found splendor: "Our walls glitter with gold—gold gleams upon our ceilings and the capitals of our pillars; yet Christ is dying at our doors in the person of his poor, naked and hungry."

We've tried to dazzle the world with the brilliance of our structures and failed. Why should the world notice when we don't look any different? But the world will notice lives of authentic abundance, rich in faith. These shine with true brilliance. We must outgrow our tedious toys that we might begin to grow our faith, and in that growing we might learn to honestly give. This is the path of contagious joy.

As we grow our faith rather than our furnishings, we find our joy in God's creation growing. Those who are inheriting the earth need not hold too tightly to any one piece of it. We soon find we have so much less to guard and so much more to give. As we become whole people, we need no longer attempt to fill our inadequacies with things. Authenticity invariably shows itself in simplicity.

We must learn the paradox of Jesus' words: "Blessed are the poor." Blessed are his poor, those who have surrendered their gods of pride, self-sufficiency and complacency. They are now free to begin the adventure of living—free to indulge in life at its fullest.

God does want us to be rich—rich in good deeds, rich in faith, rich in the marvels of his grace, rich in the wonders of his creation. With Timothy we must heed the words of Paul:

Command those who are rich in this present world not to be arrogant nor to put their hope in wealth, which is so uncertain, but to put their hope in God, who richly provides us with everything for our enjoyment. Command them to do good, to be rich in good deeds, and to be generous and willing to share. In this way they will lay up treasure for themselves as a firm foundation for the coming age, so that they may take hold of the life that is truly life. (1 Tim 6:17-19)

THE FRANTIC
GENERATION

LIVING IN AN AGE OF STRESS AND HURRY

5

Nature's cycle
Runs round and round, returning right.
But ours is running us down,
Leaving us lives without depth,
Rootless, withered, hollow husks,
Tired transplants,
No longer walking, rarely talking,
Just scurrying and
Pattering in passing.

TICKING, CLICKING, PINGING, RINGING, CHASING, RACING, CHOKing, poking—such is the pace and rhythm of modern life. At times I feel like I'm caught in a trap. Most traps prevent us from moving; this one prevents me from pausing. Even when my feet or my car isn't moving, inside I'm still churning: one more thing to do, one more errand to run, one more appointment to keep, one more overdue task to finish. I try to relax only to find my mind filled with busyness and my conscience nagging at me with details. My world whirls by in a blur of chaotic frenzy like the view from a runaway train, until I want to cry out, "Stop the world, I want to get off!"

If you have shared these feelings at times, be assured that you're not alone. It is estimated that between forty and sixty per cent of the people in our hospitals and doctors' offices are there for stress-related illness. The list of symptoms is phenomenal: heart disease, high blood pressure, ulcers, nervous breakdowns, depression, insomnia, lowered disease resistance, migraines, asthma, allergies, skin diseases and more. For others the symptoms are more subtle: a lingering fatigue, a short temper, a dull headache, an uneasy stomach, a lack of patience, a persistent restlessness. If stress is a disease, then the Western world is in the midst of a plague.

This should come as no surprise to a nation that has made busyness its cardinal virtue. How often in casual conversation do we hear "How are you doing?" answered with something like "Oh, staying busy"; "Well, you know how it is, busy as ever"; or "OK, keeping real busy"? The family may be in a shambles, health on the skids, the job bleak and dreary, but as long as we're staying busy we're presumed to be doing all right. Today's respected business people are often not the wise entrepreneurs, but the unrestrained bundles of nervous ambition, "the movers and shakers." Unfortunately, most of the moving is from one intolerable job to another, and most of the shaking is coming from a twitching hand on a coffee cup. Ulcers were once the privileged domain of the businessman, but now we've eliminated sex discrimination by extolling the "superwoman": harried married women who juggle career, family and personal life and who have made Valium this nation's leading prescription drug.

Time has indeed become our kidnaper, carrying us along

in a mad chase. I can't help but ask with Henry David Thoreau, "Why should we be in such desperate haste to succeed in such desperate enterprises?"

Regaining the Center

Have you ever had the opportunity to watch people in the woods? Those who are at home and know where they are going generally walk briskly, confidently and purposefully. But then there are those who are lost: tense and panicky, they easily break into faltering and erratic running, stumbling only to rise and run again—often in large circles. In the forest we call these people hysterical; in the city we call them ambitious.

The Frantic Generation suffers from an inward lostness as real and as devastating as this outward lostness. Foster describes this condition: "Inwardly modern man is fractured and fragmented. He is trapped in a maze of competing attachments. One moment he makes decisions on the basis of sound reason and the next moment out of fear of what others will think of him. He has no unity or focus around which life is oriented."[1]

To recover a sense of direction and pace, we need a fixed point, a known goal on which to fix our gaze, and toward which to direct our efforts. Without submitting to this unifying goal, humanity is not free, but merely random.

The English language has a word for people whose lives are not balanced around a fixed center—we call them *eccentrics*. Lack of a stable center leads to erratic, pointless activity. We need to regain a fixed center around which all the competing pieces of our fragmented lives may fall into place, an inner focus that directs and subordinates everything else. Psychologist Alfred Adler wrote: "The staking of an overall goal compels the unity of the personality in that it draws the stream of all spiritual activity into its definite direction."[2]

But where can we find a goal large enough to direct our lives? People have given themselves to various ambitions and obsessions, but any earthly pursuit, however noble, when made into a god must become a demon. Women caring only for their families have destroyed those families; men caring only for their nation's greatness have destroyed that greatness. Jesus alone gives us the calling that can sustain us, "Seek first [God's] kingdom and his righteousness" (Mt 6:33). If our faith is only one more addition to our hurried, cluttered lives, then it will only increase our stress; but if that faith stands at the very center of our being, then it provides the integrating point about which all else can take its place in harmony.

This integration brings what Jesus called purity of heart. It is the essential prerequisite to beholding God (Mt 5:8). It aligns all our motives with the truth and gives a singleness of eye (Mt 6:22). (As Søren Kierkegaard titled a book, *Purity of Heart Is to Will One Thing.*) No longer are we a battleground of competing interests. Integrity is peace. This is why Jesus can say, "Seek first his kingdom . . . and all these things will be given to you as well." Only then can we begin to live the command that we've always desired to obey: "Do not worry about tomorrow, for tomorrow will worry about itself" (Mt 6:34).

A harmonious life doesn't come immediately. We must admit our lostness and return to the path. The first step is to learn to listen.

Listening

The words of Psalm 23 are familiar to us all, but the sentiments are from a different world:

The LORD is my shepherd,
   I shall not be in want.
He makes me lie down in green pastures,
   he leads me beside quiet waters,
   he restores my soul. (vv. 1-2)

We might feel that the Lord has led us to church committees, monthly board meetings and a host of other activities, but where are the still waters? The problem is that we have become so involved in tasks and duties that we've forgotten a far more exalted task: "Be still, and know that I am God" (Ps 46:10). To begin anew we must be restored. To make God our center and his kingdom our goal, we must *listen.* Listening to God, however, is much easier to approve of than to apply in our noisy world. Exhorting a shepherd to listen is one thing; exhorting an air-traffic controller to do likewise is quite another.

To complain of constantly hearing voices was once an indication of being mad; now its merely an indication of being an American. Our Junk Generation is strewn with electronic litter; radios, stereos, televisions, loudspeakers and telephone hucksters all join together in a gigantic cacophony cajoling us to buy, believe and behave according to the latest trends. As victims of the Me Generation we seek to drown our loneliness in a sea of sound. Says Foster:

Our fear of being alone drives us to noise and crowds. We keep up a constant stream of words even if they are inane. We buy radios that strap to our wrist or fit over our ears so that if no one else is around at least we are not condemned to silence. T. S. Eliot analyzed our culture so well when he wrote, "Where shall the world be found, where will the word resound? Not here, there is not enough silence!"[3]

To effectively listen we must pull ourselves out of this swamp of static and seek quiet waters. The path to those waters will be slightly different for each of us, but each involves pausing to gain the counsel of our common Guide.

Physically we need times of rest and restoration; the same is true of our spiritual lives. Many are finding that they need extended "vacations" for this type of restoration. These vacations should be times of reorienting ourselves, times focused on listening. The academic world has long offered two- to three-month summer vacations and extended sabbaticals, and some businesses are following suit. In many European countries as well as in Canada it is common for those in a variety of professions to take extended "holidays." Those who are wearied by the routines of their profession may not need a career change so much as an extended sabbatical: anywhere from six months to five years to pursue further education or to explore other aspects of their profession, such as teaching or research. This is also a time for listening, a step back from which to re-examine career and life goals and consider any needed changes. These sabbaticals may be costly in terms of financial and career security, but they may also be investments in our sanity.

Sabbaticals are not for everyone, but annual or semiannual vacations are. A good vacation casts its relaxing shadow over the entire year as we plan and prepare for it, and then recall and relive it. We shouldn't cheat ourselves of these opportunities for listening and restoring our souls. Work and housework can wait—reviving the health and vitality of our life is more important than reviving the health and vitality of our lawn. Vacations are windows into peace once we take our eyes from the clock and take in the wonders of God's world.

Another idea is weekend or Saturday escapes (or whatever

day they may fall on). We create these pockets of time by brazenly rejecting a few of those loud imploring voices: turning off inane television programs and doing household tasks instead, turning them into times for family conversations. By paring our shopping lists to the bare essentials, we can ignore the man who is telling us to buy now and so avoid the scattered and sundry errands that consume our time. Then with those freshly redeemed days or hours, we can go and seek some silence. A path in the woods, a fishing hole or a hill in a city park can all be places for a chat with our Creator amidst his creation. The only way to waste time is to spend it doing something we don't truly believe in.

Daily vacations of twenty minutes to a half-hour are also possible. As soon as I step out the door in the morning (and quite likely well before), I'm greeted by a barrage of noise and worldly hype. If I don't have a word with God before I go, his voice may be the only one lacking in my day. What a breath of fresh air in our lives to be able to open a Gospel and listen to Jesus as he teaches hopeful crowds in Galilee, or listen to the apostle Paul as he instructs hurting Christians, or take to heart Isaiah's condemnations of his society and his promises of God's grace and restoration.

As we learn to listen, we are really learning to pray. Half of prayer is listening. There are those who can help guide us as we seek to become better listeners: O. Hallesby in *Prayer*, C. S. Lewis in *Letters to Malcolm*, Richard Foster in *Celebration of Discipline*, Brother Lawrence in *The Practice of the Presence of God* (and many other medieval thinkers such as St. Bernard, St. Theresa, St. John of the Cross), John White in *Daring to Draw Near* and others. By listening to them, we can learn to listen to God.

As the old adage says, we need to stop and smell the roses—and the spring rain and the lilacs and the pines. Every time we pause, we loosen the stranglehold that haste and hurry can have on our lives. We can utilize the naturally peaceful pauses in our day to foment a revolution of silence. Every time we stretch and smile in the fresh air or turn and laugh at a child, we unconsciously relax. Every time we affirm the harmony in creation, we take a small step toward restoring our own inner harmony. I find myself frequently pausing to notice nature: the way in which that dark green spruce is set against a deep blue sky, just as I remembered them in Colorado; the perfect way those clustered flowers bring light and softness to the shadows beneath that clump of trees, just like the rhododendrons beneath California's redwoods. Minivacations preserve the magic of longer vacations and extend them into and throughout our entire day.

We take a vacation every time we relearn the value of quiet meditation. Now as I mention meditation perhaps you picture a serene man in white sitting by a flowing stream amidst the greenery of the forest. Actually, I was thinking more of a rush-hour-bound person in a business suit sitting by a clogged onramp amidst the cloverleafs of L.A.'s expressways. Meditation is foremost a matter of attitude. Instead of becoming tense and jittery in rush-hour, muttering and honking at all those incredibly rude and inconsiderate drivers (of which we are often one), we can take the delay as an opportunity to go over our day, praying for our colleagues and planning our time. Let the car cut in; as Christians we can afford to be patient—we alone have eternity.

The purpose of all these vacations—from the macro to the micro —is to permeate our lives with peace, to create a certain stillness in which we can find refreshment and direction and in which we can listen. Yes, it does work, even in the twentieth century: it's the life God intended for us. John Fischer summed this up in a song he entitled "Still Life":

We were always meant to live a still life;
But somehow we got trapped into the fast life,
  the cast life
Where everyone plays a part.
You lose yourself in the fast life,
In the fast pace of the rat race
Where no one knows who you are,
And nobody cares.
If there really is a God
And he has something to say,
We would never hear it 'cause the noise is in the way.*

Starting Fresh

To recover our bearings in a runaway world, *planning* and *choosing* must follow listening. This is not simply something "those organized types" do. We live in a complex world, and complexity forces us to be constantly choosing—actively seeking the best. The diversity of our day opens a multitude of opportunities, but it also demands discernment of priorities. It simply won't do to "move with the herd" when we're in the midst of a stampede. To fail to set priorities is to doom ourselves to leading what Thoreau calls "lives of quiet desperation." His answer to his question of "Why should we be in such

---

STILL LIFE by John Fischer, © Copyright 1974 by LEXICON MUSIC, INC. All rights reserved. International copyright secured. Used by Special Permission.

desperate haste to succeed and in such desperate enterprises?" was to "step to the beat of a different drummer." As he said, "I came to Walden that I might live deliberately."[4] To live deliberately, to actively choose, is our inescapable human responsibility. True wisdom consists largely in recognizing priorities—not letting the noise of the immediate drown out the infinite; not letting the glare of the peripheral blind us to the crucial.

The business world provides us a good guide for our planning: the zero-based time budget. In administration a zero-based budget begins each year anew with nothing carried over from the previous year. Nothing is assumed and everything must be justified. In the same way we need to plan our life. The first step is to make a list of our priorities, the tasks that are the most important to us. If our employment involves fixed hours, we may need two lists: one for the work place and one for nonwork hours. Don't assign time periods to these tasks (you'll invariably guess wrong), but rather rank order them from the most important to the least important. Our listing of priorities should follow directly from our times of prayerful listening and reflection. Now we simply begin our day with priority number one. Rarely will there be a day in which we complete our list, but at the end of each day we can rest in the fact that what was completed was the most important. God knew what he was doing when he gave us a twenty-four-hour day; what's left over belongs to another person or another day. We can never do all that we expect ourselves to do, and we can rarely do all that others expect us to do, but we can always do all that God expects us to do. Just as we plan our tasks daily, we will need to plan our projects monthly. Do you have a day when you sit down and pay bills? Take that or some other time and also use it to plan the upcoming month.

To make zero-based planning work, three things are necessary:

First, *evaluate.* You won't get far into any management course before seeing this word. We evaluate by taking a look at our goals and our life and then seeing if the two are compatible. Almost everyone verbally agrees that people are more important than things. If we agree, the real question is, Do we devote proportionately more time to people than to things? The issue here is lifestyle integrity—are our professed priorities those which we pursue first? If someone rates time with their family above reading the sports or gossip page, then that should have some bearing on what they do first in the evening. There will be times when interruptions leave time for only one activity; the activity left for second will be the activity left undone.

Habits and addictions can sabotage our planning. We turn on the six o'clock news and then, without thinking, leave the TV on for the rest of the evening. Television appeals to our sense of loneliness and lethargy, but it merely increases both, leaving us further addicted. Living deliberately involves not only life choices but also choices about the next five minutes. Be actively choosing the best.

Second, *commit.* Commitment demands discernment. Life is made of interruptions. Even if we desired it, we cannot work in the isolation of an igloo or a monastery. Some interruptions are unavoidable: breakdowns in cars, plumbing, health and so on; these demand resourcefulness, good humor and flexibility. A result of having a relaxed, restored soul is the ability to keep things in perspective and to creatively and good-naturedly adjust schedules. Other interruptions call us to discern priorities. We should always insist on time for reflection before making any decision, whether it's buying a vacuum cleaner or joining a committee. This prevents choices based on impulse, hype, awkwardness or twisted arms. And after we make our decision, we must make sure that our yes is a yes and our no a no. No's are simple, honest admissions that we have human limitations, and yes's are direct, decisive commitments to important tasks. No longer overcommitted, we can hold steadfastly to what we have determined is important.

Finally, *pace.* Procrastination kills! It kills time, and that's the stuff our lives are made of. With any project, like swimming in the spring, the hardest part is diving in. After that, the water doesn't seem so cold. Just remember the rule: "If you must swallow a frog, don't look at it too long. If you have a number of frogs to swallow, take the big one first."

Pace for the Race

To many of us *discipline* is a dirty word, closely related to *discouraging* and *drudgery.* But discipline is at the core of discipleship. It is not drudgery because it is not an end in itself. It can be an expression of joy because it is the door to freedom. Without disciplined pacing, our lives move in fits and starts like a jalopy with a grime-clogged engine, leaving behind a trail of failed good intentions, broken promises, feverish panic, sideways skids and stalled afternoons.

We all know people who are slaves to the urgent, wearing themselves and the carpet out without ever getting anything done. They are like jack rabbits in a cactus patch with one leg shorter than the other, constantly jumping around but only going in circles. But there is an alternative, and that is to learn to run with joy and purpose. Here's how Paul describes this discipline as that of a runner in a race:

Do you not know that in a race all the runners run, but only one gets the prize? Run in such a way as to get the prize. Everyone who competes in the games goes into strict training. They do it to get a crown that will not last; but we do it to get a crown that will last forever. Therefore I do not run like a man running aimlessly; I do not fight like a man beating the air. No, I beat my body and make it my slave so that after I have preached to others, I myself will not be disqualified for the prize. (1 Cor 9:24-27)

Discipline is hard work, but what joy it will be to be able to say with Paul, "I have fought the good fight, I have finished the race, I have kept the faith. Now there is in store for me the crown of righteousness" (2 Tim 4:7-8).

To be this type of marathon runner we cannot remain jack rabbits. There's another animal running in the desert—wild horses, mustangs. When they run every sinew is striving and straining, every muscle tight and working, and yet there is no nervous stress, no frantic hurry. These mustangs run not because they are being chased, frightened or driven, but because they were born to run.

This too is our calling as Christians. Eugene Peterson takes the title for his book *Run with the Horses* from the verse in Jeremiah, "If you have raced with men on foot and they have worn you out, how can you compete with horses?" (Jer 12:5). Yes there is struggle and striving in the Christian life, but we are called to pace ourselves like the well-trained athlete, like the mustangs. Our goal in escaping the stress of the Frantic Generation is not merely to become more laid-back—a lizard lying in the sun is laid-back. Our call is not to lie with the lizards but to run with the horses. We need to regain our center and to learn to listen, plan and choose so that we may pace ourselves for the entire race, to "run in such a way as to get the prize."

Paul's words sound strange to our generation, but not impossible. Watch the lives of those rare people who are mustangs and not jack rabbits, who are active rather than just busy, who have a knack for getting things done and yet always have a spare moment for people.

Jesus was such a person. Open a Gospel and read a day in the life of Jesus. He moved through crowds healing, teaching, debating, challenging, encouraging. We see him exhausted and yet never perplexed and frantic. He still made time to intensively teach his closest followers, and he made time for quiet retreats of prayer in places of solitude. He concluded his short life with three simple words: "It is accomplished."

Look too at the lives of people like St. Francis of Assisi, Leonardo da Vinci and Benjamin Franklin. They were incredibly productive and yet they had time. "Ah, but they were geniuses," we might complain. Yes, but genius is the art of knowing what to ignore. Amidst a world of possibilities, to set forth only the best notes, brush strokes, words or experiments at the best time is wisdom. That is pacing.

Balance and Focus

Breaking free from the Frantic Generation is not an easy task.
  Timekeeper,
  Who from your hold can bring release?
  Have you a master?
  Who holds the keys to peace?
For a start we have explored a number of small but concrete steps and have considered a series of impelling "pictures"—

the galloping mustang, the disciplined athlete, the persevering apostle Paul and the indomitable Christ. We learn to bowl by counting steps and adjusting our grip and also by keeping our eyes on the pins. We learn to dance by counting steps and following patterns, but also by listening to the music.

As we begin to set goals for our days, we need to be careful to have both focus and balance. To accomplish anything we must have focus in our tasks, to hold to the main point at hand. This is not blind single-mindedness, but perseverance—maintaining the course. The key is to be interruptible—to notice the roses and to put out fires—and yet not lose our concentration amidst a barrage of static. But while focused we must also maintain balance—to not let the immediate overriding task or goal overwhelm the long-term, often more significant, goals of our lives: building our family, our faith, ourselves.

Growth in focus comes as we direct our eyes singly toward Christ, our focal point. By listening to and learning from him, we deliberately choose his best moment by moment; then we must act decisively on those choices, knowing the freedom of disciplined purpose. Wise pacing involves balance and so the following are suggestions on maintaining balance.

First, we need variety. Variety is not only the spice of life, it's the tonic for tired souls. Our days are the most relaxing and enjoyable if they have a measure of variety in their activities. For many of us that will mean getting out of our office and homes and into the out-of-doors. Instead of waiting for our upcoming vacation to get some fresh air, we can take a walk on our lunch hour. In nature we find something that is utterly indifferent to our agenda. Its cycles are its own. It will not conform to our time; we must be melded to its time. Observing nature's balance helps us restore our own. We can achieve variety in other ways as well. Instead of brooding over work problems before supper, we can play our favorite musical instrument or listen to our favorite style of music. If we've been conferring with people all day, we can plan some solitude and reading for our evening. If we've been pouring over reports all day, we can plan to get in touch with a few friends that evening. Ants can be endlessly industrious in the same task; humans need variety.

Second, we need to exercise. It's easy to overspiritualize our escape from stress, but stress is physical as well as mental and needs to be relieved by physical means. Not everyone is "athletically inclined," but the forces of our generation consistently threaten to upset the balance between rest and exertion, confining us to sedentary lives. The result is that rarely do we have the energetic sense of well-being that comes from healthy exertion. All too often we totter between dreary, droopy lethargy and restless, nervous anxiety. Coffee and its caffeine-containing cousins perk us up, but they also set our nerves on edge. Alcohol settles us down but also muddles our thinking and slows our responses. The result is that we never have energy without tension, or relaxation without drowsiness.

Exercise helps free us from this teeter-totter since it alone both stimulates blood flow and muscle tone to wake us up; it also provides an outlet for tension-causing hormones to burn nervous energy. This combination means that energy and relaxation can again be cousins, and we can begin to feel awake and alive, rested and restored. What form of exercise we choose will reflect our individual tastes, but let me again suggest variety—walking (the best place to begin), jogging, swimming, bicycling and so on. But have fun! The duty-bound Frantic Generation easily brings its frantic frenzy to its leisure:

"No pain, no gain." The Frantic Generation brings its stop-watches, and the Me Generation brings its measuring tape. But the goal is renewal—simply relearning to play.

Third, we need to be involved with people. This is the surest cure for the self-absorbed worry that can consume us. There is nothing more relaxing and reassuring than a listening ear and a helping hand. Problems become overwhelming and nerve-racking when we feel we must face them alone. Also, as we give ourselves to the great needs of others, our own stresses will seem less important. Organizing a food bank for the hungry and homeless makes it difficult to worry as intensely about whether or not we'll get that possible promotion.

Fourth, we need to learn to enjoy the process as well as the destination. Taking people climbing in the mountains, I've always been struck by the absurdity of grimly straining for three hours to attain a peak to be enjoyed for ten minutes. The trek only becomes worthwhile when its entire length is seen as an adventure to be enjoyed. I never run with a watch in my hand. When I'm out for a run, I prefer to enjoy the passing scenery and the exhilaration of movement. It is much easier to develop healthy, relaxing pacing when we're enjoying the entire process.

The Pace of Patience

Finally, we need to remember that patience is a fruit of the Spirit just as much as love. Patience is not inactivity. Our hands and feet can be flying while our hearts are patiently resting in God. In the business world people are encouraged to learn from mentors who know how to get ahead, the seasoned movers and shakers. I would suggest that we first learn from people who are seasoned veterans in the art of patience.

In a world of desperate haste, patience is the art of pacing.

Patience paces;
Haste races.

Patience says a time for everything;
Haste says time is everything.

Haste seeks to find God's kingdom;
Patience seeks to understand God's kingdom.

Haste sees the urgent;
Patience sees the important.

Haste says "So much to do!" and despairs;
Patience says "So much to do!" and delights.

Haste throws up its hands and says "Time is flying!"
Patience lifts up its hands and says "In time I'll be flying!"

Haste panics;
Patience prays.

Haste is driven;
Patience is led.

Haste seeks tomorrow and loses today;
Patience follows today and finds tomorrow.

The result of patience is to extend the peacefulness of those vacations I spoke of earlier into and throughout the entire day, to create a sense of "holy leisure." Richard Foster writes,

The church Fathers often spoke of *Otium Sanctum:* "holy leisure." It refers to a sense of balance in the life, an ability to be at peace through the activities of the day, an ability to rest and take time to enjoy beauty, an ability to pace ourselves. With our tendency to define people in terms of what they produce, we would do well to cultivate "holy leisure."[5]

Running

"Let us throw off everything that hinders and the sin that so easily entangles, and let us run with perseverance the race marked out for us. Let us fix our eyes on Jesus, the author and perfecter of our faith. . . . Consider him who endured such opposition from sinful men, so that you will not grow weary and lose heart" (Heb 12:1-3). Here is the perfect picture of disciplined pacing and single focus.

If God were to confront us as he did Jeremiah, his question might be: "If you have run the rat race and been defeated, how will you compete with horses?" The answer begins in seeking first God's kingdom. It develops through listening, planning and prioritizing. And it fills our lives through patience and perseverance. Through these we can learn that holy leisure and heroic effort are not incompatible: our feet can be racing while our hearts are resting in the One who holds the keys to peace. Run with the horses, strive with the stallions, but make it an act of joy.

THE
RESTLESS
GENERATION
LIVING IN AN AGE OF BOREDOM

6

There's a rainbow
And all of the colors are black
It's not that the colors aren't there
It's just imagination they lack
PAUL SIMON, "MY LITTLE TOWN"

THREE HITCHHIKERS WERE STRUNG OUT ALONG THE HIGHWAY holding up their destination signs. The first read "Yellowstone," and the second, "Estes Park," but the third summed up their feelings best, "Anywhere but here."

Americans are a nation on the move. Some are moving up, some moving on, some moving back; but increasingly we all seem to share a common destination: "Anywhere but here." Boredom and restlessness are certainly not new dilemmas, but never before have they so gripped entire cultures as they now do Western society.

We're going our way,
And our way is always going,
Going away.

Now we know there's no where left to go,
But we'll go,
We'll go anyway.

In the sixties the older generation had an unquenchable lust for more money and new things, and the younger generation had a similar lust for more experiences and new places. That pattern continues today, although the two generations at times exchange roles. People have always traveled and moved for the sake of adventure, but all too often the Restless Generation is motivated more by cynicism and boredom: "Anywhere but here." Never before have we possessed such mobility, but never before have our destinations seemed so unable to fill our longings. Says sociologist Jacques Ellul, "We set huge machines in motion in order to arrive nowhere."[1] Never before has a society glittered with as much diversity and variety, but never before has this variety seemed so uninspiring. "It's not that the colors aren't there; it's just imagination they lack."

We speak of being bored to death, and our words are truer than we'd like to admit. The bored die young, no matter when they're finally buried. Constantly casting off the old in search of the new, the Restless Generation steeps itself in junk. Filling yawning spaces with one more diversion and one more activity, it becomes the Frantic Generation. The great paradox of our times is how we can have so much and do so much and yet honestly enjoy so little. Perhaps it's not a paradox at all; says Robert Lee, "No wonder modern man is plagued by boredom when he flees from the drudgery of work to the meaninglessness of leisure."[2] It is the futility of meaninglessness which lies behind our restlessness. This is the irony of boredom: fitfully we fight for that missing link that will make our lives worth living only to find it melting in our grasp. Our lives become a seesaw of yearning and yawning.

Bored-Again Christians

"Now wait," you may complain, "I'm a Christian, and I've found that missing link." But does your life show it? Does your face show it? Does your faith show it? For some time Christians have mastered the art of boredom, and now it seems we've become so boring we've even bored ourselves. Yawns fill our sanctuaries on Sunday mornings. Spiritual lethargy is the curse of the church; we've become God's dozin' chosen. How true is Keith Green's lament of the church: "Jesus rose from the dead, and you can't even get out of bed." How can we affect the world when we can't keep ourselves awake?

All too often our Christian message is dry and dreary. And our Christian lives are dry and dreary. All because our view of God is dry and dreary. That is an orthodox form of blasphemy.

How different is the God of the Bible! He is the God who does amazing things in our midst. He is approached with fear and trembling, but never with yawning and stretching. The early church was accused of being crazy, but never of being boring. Worship should first and foremost be a celebration. The incredible good news is that Christ leapt up from the tomb to defeat death, and the victory party has been going on ever since!

Our world is bored because it is seeking excitement in the wrong place, searching for life in the valley of the shadow of death. We look to the church to offer us Lent—a time of stern self-deprivation. But before this we look to the world to offer us Mardi gras, Fat Tuesday, the day before Ash Wednesday when we can get in our last burst of wild, exciting living. "If we're going to spend forty days repenting, let's at least have something to repent of!" But in Rio de Janeiro where Mardi gras truly swings (New Orleans still has some catching up to do) an interesting thing has happened: the event constantly gets longer and louder, but the faces of the participants seem desperate as often as jubilant. It's the philosophy of our day, "If we could only get more . . ."

The folly in this is that all the while the true celebration is being overlooked. The true party doesn't precede Lent; it follows it. Jesus meets us Easter morning with a loaf of bread and a jug of wine and says, "These are not only the symbols of death, but also of the new abundant life for which I came. The feast is ready. Come in! Come celebrate life!"

The irony of the Restless Generation is that its members are out searching the junk heaps for scraps while ignoring the banquet that has been prepared for them. Jesus continually spoke of God's kingdom as a banquet and a wedding feast. This is a feast for all nations, a party to put the Mardi gras to shame. I've always been an adventurer at heart, but all the adventures of this world pale to insignificance before the grand adventure of coming to know the living God. "Delight yourself in the Lord," is the constant refrain of the psalmist. There are no yawns as he contemplates worship:

Then will I go to the altar of God,
   to God, my joy and my delight.
I will praise you with the harp,
   O God, my God.

Why are you downcast, O my soul?
   Why so disturbed within me?
Put your hope in God,

for I will yet praise him,
my Savior and my God. (Ps 43:4-5)

We must learn to take our delight in God; there is simply no lasting delight anywhere else. Any person and any pursuit cut off from the source of life must surely wither and die. Any pretty plum plucked from its tree soon becomes a dried-up prune. Delight begins at the source, "Delight yourself in the LORD and he will give you the desires of your heart" (Ps 37:4). Even amidst the complex attractions and distractions of our modern world we cannot escape the truth of Augustine's prayer: "Our souls are restless, Lord, until they find their rest in thee."

This is where we must all begin—again and again. Unfortunately, there are no theological secrets that will transform us into spiritual dynamos of exuberant zeal. That type of dynamic transformation only takes place in sex-appeal toothpaste commercials. The greatest saints of God all had their share of days in the doldrums. Have another look at Elijah going from calling down flames from heaven to hiding in a forgotten cave. We all run dry; what we need to discover is the resilience of faith.

God is a God of renewal. He revitalizes the old. Sings the psalmist, "He renews our strength like the eagles." Just as a middle-aged eagle sheds its plumage and grows new feathers fresh for flight, so can we. Because we have a resurrection God, we can have a resurrection faith. Being renewed, reborn, re-generated, is something that happens to us once in ultimate theological terms, but in practical terms it should be a daily occurrence. Ours is a God of fresh starts.

An exhilarating life begins with the exhilaration of a fresh view of God. This transformation begins as we see the world through the eyes of its Creator. Renewal occurs not only on the mountaintop, but also in the nitty-gritty details of daily living. Says Richard Foster, "Celebration comes when the common ventures of life are redeemed."[3]

The steps toward redeeming our days from the yawning cavities of boredom are simple (though not always easy): we need to look, serve, move, grow and celebrate. If they sound somewhat like the steps we took out of the swamp of frantic stress, that's not coincidental. The ironic truth is that boredom is often a close cousin to stress. Both are the responses of a life out of control, and both need to be tamed by regaining our focus and our balance, our direction and our pacing.

Look!

God is performing the most incredible and intricate symphony about us, a grand opera set to the music of life, and all too often we're spending our time yawning and waiting for the intermission. We should be amazed at the pageant of people and places unfolding before us. This openness and amazement can be described as "revelry," and it frequently leads to revitalization and revelation. We need to revel in the Creator as we revel in his creation.

Great are the works of the LORD;
    they are pondered by all who delight in them.
Glorious and majestic are his deeds. (Ps 111:2-3)

Tom Sine echoes the psalmist's sentiments in recalling Ransom, C. S. Lewis's character from his space trilogy. Ransom, finding himself propelled through remote space, finds it not to be the cold, dead expanse he had imagined, but rather exploding with spiritual life.

To live the good life, we need the eyes of a Ransom; we need to rediscover and celebrate the sacredness of God's creation. We need the heart of a St. Francis of Assisi to become spiritually reunited with God's good world. "The simplest and oldest way . . . in which God manifests Himself is . . . through and in the earth itself. And he still speaks to us through the earth and the sea, the birds of the air and the little living creatures upon the earth, if we can but quiet ourselves and listen." To experience the celebrative life of God we have the opportunity to take significant time not only to encounter our Creator but to become reunited with his creation in anticipation of that day when we will be harmoniously one with his new heaven and new earth.[4]

Sine goes on to describe the revelry of poor Haitians at the return of a young neighbor from a six-month absence:

They threw him up in the air. They carried him on their shoulders. They sang. They laughed. They kept Chavannes up all night partying, visiting—just enjoying him. I was envious. Usually when I return to my community, people don't even know I was gone, let alone celebrate my return.

We American Christians tend to be so caught up in our schedules, our activities, our projects, and our efforts to preserve our place at the party that we have no time left over for what was one of the central obsessions of Jesus' life—celebrating his relationships with other people. Our brothers and sisters in the Third World have much to teach us about how to put aside our quest for acquiring and possessing, and simply to relish the people around us.[5]

By pondering and delighting in nature, we revel in the wonders of God's craftsmanship. Susan often stops me to look at the silhouette of bare trees against a twilight sky or the crystalline ice patterns of a half-frozen stream. They're not the

Grand Canyon, just some old, bare trees or a trickle of water—but they're whispers of majesty.

But we also learn to look by pondering and delighting in people. Why do we idle away our hours with soap operas when the real drama of life is taking place all around us? Each person has their story, each worth hearing. "Listen to others, even the dull and the ignorant, they too have their story."

There are many wonders in our world of which we can ponder and take delight in. I am still amazed every time I have the opportunity to fly in an airliner—forget the magazine, give me a window seat! We would all do well to regain our sense of childlike wonder. What I'm speaking of again is the min-ivacation. Rather than wasted time, it is valuable time invested in learning and growing. Every time we stretch and smile in the fresh air, every time we turn and laugh at the antics of a child, every time we indulge in the wonder of life, we remove a strand of boredom. Observe, listen, study, examine, reflect, interact, ponder, delight and revel—in all these ways we can celebrate life.

Serve

Try as we may we cannot escape the great paradox of the kingdom: "Seek your life and you will lose it; lose your life and you will find it" (see Mt 10:39 and Jn 12:25). We are to lose our life in active service. All our self-seeking pursuits eventually slump into boredom. Lasting joy only comes as a caboose. We need to pour ourselves into service, and then we'll find new joys.

The exciting news about service in the kingdom is that we are significant—we can make a difference. Apathy breeds on our feelings of insignificance. This is at the root of humanity's vacillation between the drudgery of work and the meaningless-ness of leisure. A world of trivia is meaningless and a world too big leads to insignificance. But leisure invested in shaping lives is no longer meaningless, and working for kingdom goals has eternal significance; it is no longer drudgery. A national leader who changes international alliances may alter the next few years, but the ordinary Christian who changes a single heart has been used to alter eternity. There is nothing boring in this!

In broadening our vision of our world we begin to regain our perspective. As we read widely, we learn from the counsel of servants around the world. We learn also from the example of servants, whether they be Mother Teresa or our kindly Aunt Mabel. We can't let ourselves be confined by our own little world; we must learn the needs of the real world, of God's burden for that world and how we can begin to meet those needs.

Whatever way we choose to serve, we need to begin now—to give ourselves to the mission of the moment. Each person can be a light, or at least a bright spot, for one lonely heart or one cynical soul.

Move

Still waters run deep; stagnant waters run dry. The life of Jesus reminds us that we can be fruitful without being frantic. Hurry brings stress, but integrated, purposeful activity brings ac-complishment and delight.

Remember, our God is a God of renewal, and thus we can live lives of renewal, constantly becoming new persons, culti-vating new interests, finding new places. These activities take effort and we sometimes balk because we hate being beginners. But new interests also open up new worlds. Trying a new form of music, a new appreciation of art, a new sport, a new field of inquiry, or a new genre, period or style of reading can broaden us, shape us into something more than we were.

All too often bad school experiences sour us on study, and our natural curiosity dries up. We were studying grammar when we wanted to be studying creek-side frogs, and now we equate study with drudgery. But study is an activity that opens the doors of discovery, and we shouldn't allow reluctance to rob us of the initial exhilaration and the lasting satisfaction of discovery.

Any relationship—with a friend, a spouse, a parent or child, or with God—is a purposeful activity that takes initiative and creativity. Good relationships are dynamic: to remain alive they must grow. We need to invest time and imagination in others to truly enjoy the fullness of fellowship. Without this commitment our relationships wither into boredom.

A growing relationship with God is no less active than any other interpersonal relationship. At the core of this relationship is worship, and vital worship begins when we are alone with God. We can find new places, times and ways to pray. We can be creative in Bible study, wrestling in new ways with the events, people and themes of Scripture. Building on this, we can worship with our family, roommates or small groups. We can begin to have imaginative group devotions by singing, reading to each other, discussing issues and problems, telling stories, doing skits, praying.

And we can revitalize our worship as a church. Ever wonder what the largest spectator sport in America is? It's Christianity. When we only watch and judge the performance of a select few, of course we become bored again. But Christianity isn't a performance to be viewed and approved; it's a divine drama, a passion play in which we're all vital supporting actors. We should think of ourselves as participants in the church service and not as mere observers. We can spend musical interlude times in prayer and worship, not judging hair styles. We can come early and read a hymn, psalm or selection of liturgy to focus our thoughts. Or we can stay late and welcome newcomers and encourage old-timers.

Our worship should be a time of celebration. Our creativity is a gift of God, and we are to share it with him. But a word of caution: I'm not speaking of zealous emotionalism (that is the Junk Generation at worship), nor of endless committee-bound duties (that is the Frantic Generation at work), but of honest, jubilant celebration overflowing into honest, committed service.

Grow

The rich fool of whom Jesus speaks (Lk 12) has his counterparts in the bored generation. Their wealth grows day by day and their possessions abound while their minds grow narrower, their hearts smaller and their spirits frailer. Eventually they lose the capacity to enjoy even the least of what they accumulate. They remind us that it doesn't matter how big our barns are, but how big we are. The expansive life need not be an expensive life. For a bigger world we need only a broader vision. It matters little how much we have; what's important is how much we enjoy.

Foster writes:
Superficiality is the curse of our age. The doctrine of instant satisfaction is a primary spiritual problem. The desperate need today is not for a greater number of intelligent people,

or gifted people, but for deep people.[6]

Growth comes through looking, serving and moving, but it takes discipline. Our impatience dooms us to superficiality; we don't take the time to develop our friendships, our abilities, our interests. We don't make the concerted effort to get below the surface, and so in time we become bored with the shallowness of our lives. To get beneath the surface we need to become deeper persons, developing all that with which God has entrusted us. In C. S. Lewis's *The Chronicles of Narnia*, he has this marvelous exchange between Lucy, a young girl, and Aslan, a great lion who is a figure of Christ:

"Welcome, child," he said.

"Aslan!" said Lucy, "you're bigger."

"That is because you are older, little one," answered he.

"Not because you are?"

"I am not. But every year you grow, you will find me bigger."[7]

Celebrate

"Rejoice in the Lord always. I will say it again: Rejoice!" (Phil 4:4).

Be thankful. Let the word of Christ dwell in you richly as you teach and admonish one another with all wisdom, and as you sing psalms, hymns and spiritual songs with gratitude in your hearts to God. And whatever you do, whether in word or deed, do it all in the name of the Lord Jesus, giving thanks to God the Father through him. (Col 3:15-17)

For some of us this talk of celebration and joy seems like a foreign language or an impossible dream. Part of the reason for this is what C. S. Lewis calls the "law of undulation." We will never escape the pendulum swings of our emotions as long as we live in an earthly time frame, for shifts in mood, with occasional lows, are simply part of our emotional make-up. It is the nature of these lows to convince us at the time that they're here to stay, but they rarely ever are. Gloom need not be our captor. As we grow our faith, we develop resilience. Active thanksgiving produces perseverance. Others, however, may find themselves the prisoner of a more serious captor, and that is apathy.

It may seem strange that I've dealt with the various aspects of boredom in our society and have only mentioned in passing the most commonly cited affliction of today's generation: apathy. This is because boredom and apathy are slightly different diseases. Boredom is atrophy of the emotions; apathy is atrophy of the will. Our first response to boredom is restlessness: seeking satisfaction in junk, in material clutter, or in frantic activity. When these fail to nourish us the disease may become more serious. Apathy begins in narrow individualism and ends in cold cynicism, which will be explored in the next chapter.

The answer to both apathy and boredom begins in actively and thankfully receiving the abundant life that is in Christ. His message remains the same, "I have come that [you] may have life, and have it to the full" (Jn 10:10). This is the new perspective that we need. We seek all things so that we might enjoy life; Christ gives us life that we might enjoy all things. We restlessly seek a life of abundance; Christ offers an abundance of life.

As we grow through looking, serving and becoming involved, we open ourselves to thankfully receiving this gift of life. This is a sure way to be a beacon for our twisted and warped generation. Nothing will so attract a bored world as the shine of honest joy, someone who is what Spanish-speakers call "llena de vida"—full of life, filled with God's abundant life. Life is God's precious gift to us, his grand display of his creative genius. We are to celebrate it to the fullest, and let a dull world hear the sound of the music. "The banquet is ready, come celebrate life!"

THE
HOLLOW
GENERATION

LIVING IN AN AGE OF
CYNICISM

7

Remember us—if at all—not as lost
Violent souls, but only
As the hollow men
The stuffed men.
T. S. ELIOT, "THE HOLLOW MEN"

They are clouds without rain, blown along by the wind;
autumn trees, without fruit and uprooted—twice dead. They
are wild waves of the sea, foaming up their shame; wandering
stars, for whom blackest darkness has been reserved forever.
JUDE 12-13

JUDE'S IMAGINATIVE DESCRIPTION OF THE MEN OF HIS TIME
seems to apply strikingly to a group popular today—the cynics—whom Eliot terms "the hollow men." History has always
known its cynics, but rarely has cynicism so tinged and col-
ored every aspect of a society's thinking. Today, to be optimis-
tic is to be naive; to be informed is to be cynical. The Buddha's
mark of enlightenment was a placid smile; the modern West-
erner's mark is a sneer.

For some, cynicism is philosophical. Around the turn of the century, those disenchanted by what they saw of organized religion turned hopefully to liberal humanism, which sought to build a new society. For all their differences, Christianity and this revived humanism had one thing in common—they both offered hope.

But these new thinkers claimed that in looking over the past nineteen hundred years Christianity has proved itself inadequate to the task. And yet in the wake of two brutal world wars, oppressive political regimes, attempted genocide and economic depression, this new humanism took only thirty years to reach the same fate. Humanism lost faith in its own optimism and was replaced by the philosophy of despair—existentialism. From Picasso to Sartre and Camus, it was agreed that, if meaning was to exist at all, it had to be manufactured. Their predecessor, Nietzsche, had buried God; now they dug a grave next door for hope. The intellectuals had joined the ranks of the cynical.

The general population in the United States didn't give up so easily. The depression and war years were followed by the economic idealism of the fifties. When that dream proved hollow, it was replaced by the social idealism of the sixties. When that dream grew anemic, there was a return to economic emphases, but the idealism was never revived; this was cold, hard, push-to-the-top economic survival. Presidents went from being hailed as heroes to being accepted as the lesser of two evils. Social reform became get-yours movements. All agreed that war was a futile monstrosity, but war didn't end. All agreed that society was unjust, but society didn't change. Based on experience, the general populace joined the ranks of the cynics. Cynicism was survival.

The Descent of Man

To understand how cynicism has pervaded our thinking, we need only look at the modern view of the present, of the future and of humanity.

The teacher of Ecclesiastes was ahead of his time.

"Meaningless! Meaningless!"
    says the Teacher.
"Utterly meaningless!
    Everything is meaningless." (Eccles 1:2)

Much of the modern view of the present is a lament of its meaninglessness. Psychoanalyst Carl Jung said, "The central neurosis of our time is emptiness." And what he saw was only the beginning. Albert Einstein observed, "Perfection of means and confusion of goals characterize our age." Said Sartre in *Nausea,* "I was just thinking that here we are, all of us, eating and drinking to preserve our precious existence, and there's nothing, nothing, absolutely no reason for existing." In this context Ecclesiastes sounds surprisingly modern:

I thought in my heart, "Come now, I will test you with pleasure to find out what is good." But that also proved to be meaningless. "Laughter," I said, "is foolish. And what does pleasure accomplish?" . . . What does a man get for all the toil and anxious striving with which he labors under the sun? All his days his work is pain and grief; even at night his mind does not rest. This too is meaningless. (Eccles 2:2-3, 22-23)

Both leisure and work have become meaningless. We seek countless diversions from this emptiness, only to find our diversions losing their meaning. Activities and goals emptied of meaning are also emptied of value. Perhaps Oscar Wilde said it best, "What is a cynic? A man who knows the price of everything and the value of nothing."

Disgust with the present is nothing new, but it has always been tempered by hope for the future. Stripped of that hope we stand naked indeed. Blaise Pascal asked a question about the cynics of his day that speaks even louder of ours: "What will become of men who despise little things, and do not believe great ones?" The answer perhaps lies in the words of Ingersoll, the acclaimed cynical critic of Christianity. In the end he abandoned his biting wit to conclude soberly with these words: "Life is a narrow vale between two cold and barren peaks. We strive to see beyond them and cry out for an answer, but the only response is the echo of our own wailing."

There is one final step to cynicism. Cynicism about the present and the future can become cynicism about humanity itself. Jacob Bronowski boldly proclaimed *The Ascent of Man* in his best-selling book. But when he turned to *The Identity of Man* and what makes us fundamentally different from machines, he could only grasp at straws unworthy of his scholarship. We are machines by birth, he concluded, but persons by experience. But if experience gives us our personhood and that experience proves meaningless, then what can we say? The third grave has been dug for humanity itself, and cynicism is complete. We are only machines, so they say, and naturally we become just that.

Fighting Frostbite
But why should we live like lifeless machines when the world is full of radiant life! Creation cries out with vibrancy and invites us to rise above our gloomy philosophies. We seek hope but are offered cheap imitations: voices from beyond the grave, mystics and spiritualists, astrologers and sensational in-

terpreters of prophecy. The average person has the supermarket tabloids and the intellectuals have Sartre's *Nausea*. Neither has any meaningful or lasting hope.

But what about those who claim a living hope? We too must be careful because cynicism kills in the manner of frostbite: the only symptom is a deadening numbness. And even Christians are often tinged with this frostbite. Callousness and doubt numb us to life and joy. We find ourselves leaving the triumphant lyrics of the old hymns on the church doorstep, because they appear hopelessly out of step with the world waiting outside. Our problem is not that we've been taught to question our faith, but rather that we've been taught to reject any answers. Doubt can be a state of mind—or it can be a way of life.

The good news of the incarnation and resurrection sounds continually more and more unpalatable, not because they've been disproven but because we've become suspicious of any good news. We blush at presenting the gospel. It somehow seems childish; not because it's intellectually unsound, but because it's a message of hope and today only children have unbounded hope. Only old Walt Disney movies have happy endings; in adult movies the hero bleeds to death in the sewer.

Cynicism, however, is not the only honest response to our broken world. Hope is not vain idealism, but an honest response to the fact of God's grace. As Christians our eyes need not be closed, but wide open to see the whole story. In *Running from Reality*, Michael Green writes,

A truly Christian humanism makes room both for hope and for realism about man and his world. Hope because the Christian believes in God, Creator, Saviour, Indweller. This God cared for us enough to become one of us: he will not scrap our world. There is room for optimism, if you believe in God. Equally the Christian humanist is a realist, well aware, as his scriptures no less than his observation tell him, of fallen human nature. He wears no rose-tinted spectacles about the goodness of mankind, and the virtues of either the aristocracy or the proletariat. He knows that, left to themselves, people are incurably selfish. The cross reminds him of what human wickedness is capable of. The resurrection reminds him of how God can overrule it.[1]

Our world, although fallen, still shines with radiant life because it reflects the life of the one in whom all things hold together. We can joyously do the same. We can cease being somber and begin to believe great things. Healed, we can become healers. But we need more than new and improved packages of evangelistic techniques; we need to cease conforming to this world; we need to be transformed by the renewing of our minds. Os Guinness sums up our situation, "Modern ecclesiastics and ancient Ecclesiastes come around to the same conclusion: Leave out God and the high demands of his ways, and we soon find we have exchanged the 'holy of holies' for 'vanity of vanities.' "[2] True hope only comes packaged with faith and love. Only by growing a living faith and living a growing love can we ever lay claim to a lasting hope.

The Backbone of Faith

Cynicism isn't a bad beginning. It's a terrible ending. Of course things of this world never satisfy us. They were never meant to. Anything in this world when given our first devotion crumbles. But that is when we must look beyond this world. It's good that we're learning to despise cheap answers, but we must then be willing to replace them with great things.

Christianity does not provide easy answers. The Bible is not an endless, empty tale of smiles, and neither should we be. The Old Testament is often brutally blunt. The New Testament takes us first to the cross and only then to the resurrection.

We may begin in brokenness, but beyond the empty tomb we can cry with Psalm 118, "In my anguish I cried to the LORD, and he answered by setting me free" (v. 5). Our hope is real—as flesh and blood as our Savior, as concrete as an empty tomb. Without this, *hope* is an empty word. We have a living hope only because we have a living Savior. We are born "into a living hope through the resurrection of Jesus Christ from the dead" (1 Pet 1:4).

We are called to be tough, but never calloused. Insects have a hard outer shell since their soft and vulnerable inner parts need protection. It's also the skeletal structure of the cynic. But with our faith as a backbone we have inner strength and so we have no need for outer hardness. We must never deny the reality of our broken world (the Bible certainly does not), and yet we are called not "to grieve like the rest of men, who have no hope" (1 Thess 4:13). Instead, "We are hard pressed on every side, but not crushed; perplexed, but not in despair; persecuted, but not abandoned; struck down, but not destroyed" (2 Cor 4:8-9).

"Perplexed, but not in despair"—this isn't fantasy but grace. Says Paul,

We have gained access by faith into this grace in which we now stand. And we rejoice in the hope of the glory of God. Not only so, but we also rejoice in our sufferings, because we know that suffering produces perseverance; perseverance, character; and character, hope. And hope does not disappoint us, because God has poured out his love into our hearts by the Holy Spirit, whom he has given us. (Rom 5:2-5)

What we need in order to face the future confidently and to develop joyful perseverance is to more fully come to know the extent, depth and richness of the love of God in Christ.

Cynics never tire of trying to see *beyond* our precious ideals— *Beyond Good and Evil* (Nietzsche), *Beyond Freedom and Dignity* (Skinner)—but no one can get beyond the love of God. It is the one precious ideal that can never fail us. All the adventures of this world pale to insignificance before the grand adventure of coming to know the living God. The cynics were right about three things: nothing in this world merits our utterly devoted allegiance; nothing in this world can fill our longings; and nothing in this world will never fail us. But as C. S. Lewis pointed out, our longings, hopes and desires point to realities just as hunger points to food. Living hope rests in a vision of the living God and an understanding of the grace of his living Christ and is a gift of his Holy Spirit. Nothing else will satisfy. Nothing else was meant to.

The Touch of Love

How do we argue against a mindset that has pronounced all arguments futile and all answers empty? Michael Green describes our dilemma: "There is something very strange about the opposition to Christianity. It is not usually direct or reasoned. It is snide and cynical; it comes with a laugh or a groan. 'You're not one of that lot, are you?' "[3]

Though sometimes hostile, cynicism can also be a cry for help. For all of the intellectual veneer, few people turn philosophically to cynicism without first arriving at its conclusions experientially. In the eighteenth century Voltaire described the dilemma of one whose thinking only led to skepticism. He could still choose his actions, but failed; futile action led to anguish; and inaction led to ennui—meaningless boredom. Voltaire's only solution was a motto for our day: "Tend your own garden." Cynicism is insulation from the pain of life. Pain leads to suspicion, apathy and isolation. For these reasons cynics cannot just be told about hopeful living, they must see it.

Just as cynicism can spread and nip Christians with frost-bite, so Christian faith should grow out and thaw the cynic. To do this, we need not present a sea of synthetic smiles, but frank, sincere honesty. Suspicion, apathy and isolation are overcome by insight, patience and forgiveness.

Insight

Cynics accuse the faithful of having committed intellectual suicide, but those whom cynicism has drawn into the slough of spiritual apathy have committed volitional suicide. They have surrendered the will to probe beneath the debris of a broken world to discover the original treasure that still lies beneath. Cynicism can use apathy as an escape from reality. It is the cynic who misconstrues reality by refusing to see the whole picture. Yes it's terrible that Down's syndrome children are born with a misplaced chromosome, but first we need to see the inexplicable, awe-inspiring interaction of the twenty-two perfect pairs of chromosomes before we talk about what's out of order with the twenty-third.

Insight is the art of seeing below the surface, actively view-ing the world. This is not merely "looking on the bright side." Insight begins in objectivity, not sentimentality. Insight de-mands that we look at problems head on, but also that we do not become myopic. We must see both the loving creation that lies behind and the glorious redemption that lies ahead.

To become a person of insight we need to dig deep. For instance, we can read Philippians to understand the basis of Paul's rejoicing amidst hardship. We can grapple with Habakkuk and Job as they cry "Why?" and follow Isaiah as he goes from turmoil to hope.

But we need to do more than just study the Bible. We need to become involved in the world. As we read the morning newspaper we can't be content with skimming over its catalog of atrocities and abuses. We need to learn also of how God's people are working to heal those hurts and correct injustices and see where we can become involved.

Insight depends on knowledge. We should learn the historical, psychological, scientific and philosophical basis of our faith (at whatever level is appropriate). Books by C. S. Lewis (perhaps the most insightful apologist of this century), G. K. Chesterton and Michael Green can be good places to start. Our goal is not to develop the pat answers to win arguments, but to develop the confidence to win respectful attention.

The cynic must be reminded of William Penn's warning, "Don't despise what you don't know." This danger is echoed in Jude 10: "These men speak abusively against whatever they do not understand." Although this is human nature, our call is to gently and thoughtfully explain ourselves: "Always be prepared to give an answer to everyone who asks you to give the reason for the hope that you have. But do this with gentleness and respect" (1 Pet 3:15). We can encourage others by our example to probe beneath the surface, to earnestly cultivate insight.

Patience
Both the cynic and the Christian often face situations beyond their control. Faced with such a situation, we can respond with either patience or resignation.

Patience embraces hope;
Resignation replaces hope.

Patience is a stillness of heart;
Resignation is a deadness of heart.

Patience prays;
Resignation sighs.

Patience says, "I'm on my way";
Resignation says, "There is no way."

Patience finds its strength mounting daily;
Resignation finds its strength ebbing daily.

Patience says, "We've just begun . . ."
Resignation says, "It's all over .   "

Patience rests the soul;
Resignation robs the soul.

Patience understands limitations;
Resignation limits understanding.

Patience waits and tries;
Resignation hates and dies.

Confronted with a world that at times seems overwhelming, all of us can feel insignificant and frail. But we must remember that "God chose the weak . . . to shame the strong" (1 Cor 1:27). Our feelings of weakness force us to look to him who promises: "My grace is sufficient for you, for my power is made perfect in weakness" (2 Cor 12:9). And so we can say with confidence, "For when I am weak, then I am strong" (2 Cor 12:10). Seeing ourselves as insignificant cogs in a vast machine that is going nowhere leads to apathetic resignation, but realizing that we are integral blocks in the building of God's kingdom allows us to work and to wait.

Jesus compared God's kingdom to a mustard seed, which though it is the smallest of seeds, in time grows into a bountiful tree. Tom Sine uses this parable in his book *The Mustard Seed Conspiracy* to show how the church can make a difference in a troubled world. He concludes by telling the story of an old shepherd in the Provence region of southern France, which by 1913 had been left desolate through poor farming practices and abuse of the land. The shepherd's response was to begin planting trees. He was chided for putting so much effort into something whose benefits he might never see. But his response was, "Perhaps my children will." Years later, travelers were amazed at the transformation of the land and the restoration of its forests, wildlife, agriculture and population. The old shepherd was honored even by the Chamber of Deputies for bringing the valley once again back to life. Sine concludes,

The old shepherd had lived to see the seeds he planted transform an entire region. Not everyone may be so fortunate. But we should never underestimate the difference the insignificant can make. A seed or a life, planted in love, can bring surprising change. As you have seen in these pages,

God is transforming the world through the conspiracy of the insignificant. In every place, time, and culture he is planting his seeds in this barren earth. And they are bringing new life, new hope, and a new beginning for his people and his world.[4]

The vitality of our lives can be eroded and laid bare like the French region mentioned above. The way of restoration begins in the planting of seeds. Through a life of purposeful, patient activity, we can introduce the cynical world around us to God's kingdom, which begins as tiny as a mustard seed, but grows to embrace the skies.

Forgiveness

While we have clouded this word with unrealistic sentimentality and subtle evasions, the New Testament word for forgiveness has a simple root: to let go. We cling to the hurts of the past, reliving bitter experiences, shadow boxing with adversaries long gone, evening scores that have long since been erased. In the end we are only trapped by the iron grip of our own resentment. We need to learn to let go. To forgive is to be set free from the pain of the past, to press on ahead renewed and restored. Jacques Rossel writes,

Only the proclamation of forgiveness, which allows new beginnings, can lift up the drooping hands and strengthen the weak knees (Heb. 12:12). It alone can give courage to the discouraged; it alone can enable one to face one's self and accept one's mistakes and faults. Forgiveness starts off the movement of love which our disobedience is always compromising. . . . It alone provides a sound basis for hope in the midst of the situations of despair. It alone enables men to go forward and truly progress.[5]

The first thing we need to let go of is our claims on God. Not that he needs our forgiveness, but we need the release. Our beautiful world is twisted, and that means it never quite meets our expectations. When that happens we cry out, "It's not fair!" Of course not. Who promised us it would be? It's not fair that many of us go to sleep at night in a warm bed with a full stomach while thousands of others are dying from war and starvation. Nothing in our lives is fair—it is all grace! We have no claim on our world, no claim on God to deliver; every breath of our lives is sheer grace.

There are painful times in our lives, some terribly so. Those times call for insight, for patience—and for weeping. In our controlled society we're losing the ability to grieve, and grief is a much better alternative than lingering bitterness. If we take the time to grieve, we may never know the totality of despair. Weep with those who weep, and then together turn to the Comforter who weeps with us all. There is a season for sorrow, but then comes the letting go. "Blessed are those who mourn, for they will be comforted" (Mt 5:4). But woe to those who refuse to be comforted, for they have condemned themselves. God is with us in our pain as well in our joy, and God's fellowship always brings comfort. Honestly accepting both our hurt and his comfort, we can begin the healing of memories.

The second thing we can do is to forgive ourselves. Everyone has been cold, calloused, blind and downright stupid in the past. That's part of being a member of fallen humanity. God could take stock of our lives and come up with a much longer list. But he never does. When we ask, he forgives—it's his specialty. To refuse to accept that free forgiveness is to call God a liar. Yes, in the past I've done some mighty stupid things, but God has forgiven them and others have forgotten them;

it's time I do as well. The most wasted conversations are rehearsals of what we should have said. Don't allow paying for the past to impoverish the present. Guilt is helpful only as a guide to lead us to the Forgiver. If we face him and, if possible, face those we may have hurt and find the freedom of those almost forgotten words, "Will you forgive me?" then we can leave the burden behind us. When we let go of the past, we have both hands free to embrace the future.

The final step in letting go is to forgive others. When we've been hurt we have three options. The first is judgment and revenge. We're determined to get even, even if we have to do it in our minds. We dredge up again and again the single act of cruelty or indifference, and that single wound becomes surrounded by a score of self-inflicted wounds. Why do we love to dwell on offenses? Sometimes it is easier to hate than to hurt, to rage than to weep. There is energy in hatred; it can drive us on. And anger can make us feel righteous. Our self-esteem is bolstered by our martyrdom. But whatever we receive from this judgmental hatred, we must realize that in time it turns in on ourselves. "As we judge, so we are judged." The process, as C. S. Lewis describes it, is this:

Suppose one reads a story of filthy atrocities in the paper. Then suppose that something turns up suggesting that the story might not be quite true, or not quite so bad as it was made out. Is one's first feeling, "Thank God, even they aren't quite so bad as that," or is it a feeling of disappointment, and even a determination to cling to the first story for the sheer pleasure of thinking your enemies as bad as possible? If it is the second then it is, I am afraid, the first step in a process which, if followed to the end, will make us into devils. You see, one is beginning to wish that black was a little blacker. If we give that wish its head, later on we shall wish to see grey as black, and then to see white itself as black. Finally, we shall insist on seeing everything—God and our friends and ourselves included—as bad, and not be able to stop doing it, we shall be fixed for ever in a universe of pure hatred.[6]

The second option is no better. That is denial. We insulate ourselves with a hard, calloused aloofness that is impenetrable. Do you remember the Simon and Garfunkel song "I Am a Rock"? The singer takes comfort in the fact that a rock "feels no pain" and "never cries." But neither does a rock ever know joy. We cannot escape C. S. Lewis's warning, "Hell is the only place outside of heaven where we can be safe from the dangers of love."[7]

We are left then with the third option, forgiveness: to readily and honestly admit that we've been hurt, to consider the cause and then to lay it aside. To let go. Forgiveness does not say, "It was nothing" (that's denial), but "Yes it hurt; now how can we repair the damage?" Forgiveness is surrendering our supposed right to even the score. It is giving up our claim to remind and chide, to parade our wounds. To truly live in the present we must release our death grip on the past.

Too often we limit our concept of forgiveness to resolving raging feuds. But unforgiveness doesn't always shake its fist and warn, "I'll get even"; often it clenches up inside in a tight fist and says to itself, "I will never again . . " This hardness of heart, which cuts us off from the offending party, can in the long run be even more destructive.

Sandie was a seemingly well-adjusted and successful, if a bit quiet, young woman. Her life, however, had a deep-seated sadness that showed itself most clearly during the holiday season when she became depressed. Unable to make peace with her childhood where she was verbally abused, she remained unable to make peace with her caring but rigid, hypercritical father. As a child she withdrew from his stern disapproval to the safety of her own room, a pattern that was all the easier when as a grown woman her room was an apartment across town. He remained unable to forgive "failure" and she remained unable to forgive his unforgiving rigidity. The result was a buried hurt that separated her not only from her father, but to receiving care and love from anyone. Her outwardly capable cynicism held her inwardly captive to loneliness. Their relationship remained hospitable and civil, yet strained and aloof—until his heart attack broke their hardness of heart. As he went through several stages of by-pass surgery, he had to face his own weakness, and she had to admit the love and compassion that remained beneath her calloused wounds. Once they were able to admit these to each other, they were on their way to healing. For them it took the edge of death to bring life back into their relationship.

When withdrawal has taken place, forgiveness involves breaking down walls, letting go of rigid self-reserve and, like the father of the prodigal son, running earnestly toward the estranged person and with tears exclaiming, "What was dead is now alive! What was lost is found!" This type of forgiveness can be terrifying and it can be awkward, but it also brings new life to relationships that have become frozen wastes, and it brings healing to the frostbitten people in them. "Behold, I make all things new" (Rev 21:5 RSV).

A Cynic's Psalm
Grounded in faith and growing in insight, patience and for-

giveness, we can model true hope. Longfellow describes these sentiments in his "Psalm of Life":

Tell me not, in mournful numbers,
Life is but an empty dream!—
For the soul is dead that slumbers,
And things are not what they seem.

Life is real! Life is earnest!
And the grave is not its goal:
Dust thou art, to dust returnest,
Was not spoken of the soul.

But don't expect a cynical world to be quickly roused. Frost-bitten parts must be warmed slowly. Without gentleness and respect we are more likely only to do further damage, and to further alienate the cynic.

No, my long winded fellow,
Spare me your rousing rhythms
Spun from your life of pampered ease.
It is folly to sing a psalm of life
To one already twice dead.
You cannot know the persistence of my pain,
How the soul that is dying never slumbers.
Enough lilac lyrics,
Put down your pen!
And tell me of the man of fewer words
Who died forsaken, and then
Rose again.

Easter is the message of hope amidst hopelessness. Have another look at the risen Jesus walking with two sullen, broken

122

disciples on the road to Emmaus (Lk 24:13-35). He patiently reveals the message of the Scriptures, which give insight into the real significance behind the seemingly hopeless events surrounding the crucifixion. What had seemed to be a bitter ending was in fact a new beginning. Renewed and forgiven, the two men were finally then able to recognize their risen Lord. Through the patient honesty of our life and words, we can guide those in the cynical world to that same recognition. There is hope in no one else.

COURIERS
OF THE
KINGDOM

LIVING AUTHENTICALLY IN
AN AGE OF HYPE

8

*We are not meant to remain as children at the mercy
of every chance wind of teaching, and of the jockeying of men
who are expert in the crafty presentation of lies.
But we are to speak the truth in love, and to grow up
in every way into Christ, the head.*
EPHESIANS 4:14-15 (PHILLIPS)

I KNOW OF A HAMBURGER STAND WHERE EVERY YEAR THE SIGN gets bigger and the hamburgers get smaller. I can't help but wonder if someday it won't be all sign and no burger.

That hamburger stand characterizes the modern world. We call it hype. We live in the age of the public relations person. Manufacturers manufacture their own "scientific" studies; politicians seek to rewrite history to their own advantage; and the vast power of the media has been used to turn our lives into a giant commercial. We once saw ourselves as the land of promise, but now we've become merely the land of promises.

success." In the last televised presidential debate the crucial, final preparation immediately before the debate was not brushing up on foreign policy but choosing the correct color and pattern of the candidate's tie. As a sales manager once counseled me, "Don't sell the steak—sell the sizzle." This appears to be the wisdom of our day. We look to pop singers as our social commentators, fashion models as our newscasters, actors as our national leaders, and football players as our theologians. Some succeed in their newfound roles and for the others it doesn't really matter, because we no longer expect them to be leaders, heroes or geniuses—only celebrities.

Eugene Peterson sums up this pattern strikingly:

If . . . we look around for what it means to be a mature, whole, blessed person, we don't find much. These people are around, maybe as many of them as ever, but they aren't easy to pick out. No journalist interviews them. No talk show features them. They are not admired. They are not looked up to. They do not set trends. There is no cash value in them. No Oscars are given for integrity. At year's end no one compiles a list of the ten best-lived lives.[1]

Even the church has bowed to hype. Driving into Denver I was amazed that the largest billboards lining the freeway were advertising a single church. A sign in a Christian bookstore espoused modern doctrine: "Proclaim your faith, buy a bumper sticker." Much is said today about the problems of the church, but I believe its greatest problem is a simple one: so many believers, so few disciples. The church always needs greater resources, but above all it needs greater integrity.

From Hype to Hope

Integrity is more than honesty—it is having our entire being aligned with the truth. Under *integrity* Webster lists five synonyms: soundness, incorruptibility, completeness, honesty and unity. Integrity comes from a Latin word meaning "whole or entire, that which is untouched." This idea of wholeness and honest simplicity (which modern psychologists have picked up on under terms such as "congruence") is an ancient idea with strong biblical affinity. Jesus strikingly described it as purity of heart and singleness of eye. In today's cluttered confusion it is an important concept to revive. Bonhoeffer describes it this way: "To be simple is to fix one's eye solely on the simple truth of God at a time when all concepts are being confused, distorted and turned upside-down."[2]

Integrity allows us to see clearly: "If your eye is sound, your whole body will be full of light" (Mt 6:22 RSV); "Blessed are the pure in heart, for they will see God" (Mt 5:8). Plato went so far as to say that "beauty depends on simplicity—I mean the true simplicity of a rightly ordered mind and character." To be a person of integrity is to have inner simplicity, to have an inner soundness that is uncorrupted, untouched by the shams of our day. It is to be authentic in a world of hype.

How do we achieve this integrity? Jesus offered only one way: "Love the Lord your God with all your heart and with all your soul and with all your mind and with all your strength" (Mk 12:30). This is the key to integrity—to have all our faculties focused in a single direction. Again we are confronted by the great paradox of the kingdom: only in losing ourselves in seeking God do we find ourselves; only in admitting our brokenness before him are we made whole. "Blessed are the poor in spirit, for theirs is the kingdom of heaven" (Mt 5:3).

Hype plays on our fearful pride; integrity comes only to

those who have found the freedom of carefree humility. Believe it or not, humility is actually fun! Humility is light, it's easy, and it's liberating. There's no drearier burden than pride; in the end it drains our very life.

Pride uses its talents to impress others;
Humility uses its talents to bless others.

Pride looks in mirrors;
Humility looks at others.

Pride is ever anxious;
Humility is at ease with itself.

Pride is constantly embarrassed;
Humility laughs a lot.

Pride impresses new aquaintances;
Humility enjoys old friends.

Pride wins fleeting admiration;
Humility wins lasting love.

Pride builds dividing walls;
Humility never notices them

Pride looks inward and stumbles;
Humility looks outward and dances.

Pride broadcasts its virtuous actions;
Humility is too busy with them to bother.

Pride wearies under its own weight;
Humility travels light and goes the second mile.

Pride seeks praise;
Humility praises.

Pride seeks itself and in the end is left alone;
Humility forgets itself, and in the end inherits the kingdom.

Taking Out the Trash

Humility is the foundation of integrity Humility frees us from vain pursuits. Ever-increasing junk, self-indulgence, clutter and frantic activity are merely vain attempts to fill the holes in our lives. Those in the rat race are running on a treadmill. When our vain pursuits fail to keep their inflated promises, we are left restless and cynical. Humble simplicity is emptying ourselves of the trash that fills our lives so that God may fill us with his abundant life. For those trapped in counterfeit lives, Christ still offers his great promise: "You will know the truth, and the truth will set you free" (Jn 8:32). Authentic integrity comes as we explore broadly, speak directly and live wholeheartedly.

Explore broadly. Jesus confronted his disciples for calling him teacher (rabbi) and yet paying so little attention to what he said. Being disciples means being students of the Teacher, continually learning from him and continually reflecting on our world. This entails first of all that we are to be "people of the Book," studying the Bible meditatively, prayerfully, intellectually and deeply.

But we should be both students of the Word and students of the world. We need to reject trivia, hype and prepackaged simplifications. To avoid having our minds shackled to the shallowness of superficial hype we need to grow in height (the intellectual dimension), in depth (the historical dimension) and in breadth (the cultural dimension). This does not take great intellect, but great interests.

Every day we are presented with many opportunities for learning. We often don't need to go far for a crosscultural experience. Our cities and countrysides are places of incredible diversity, but all too often interstate highways usher us hurriedly from one familiar setting to its look-alike somewhere else. We need to avoid being blinded by the familiar and to get out, observe and reflect on what we see and hear. Our task is to analyze and act instead of just to observe and absorb. This book only touches on a few of the issues Christians need to confront. There are many others—racism, the pervasiveness of violence, glorified nationalism—that I've left as beyond the scope of this book. But these issues and others need our informed response. No we can't all become experts on everything, but like the French shepherd we can all begin to plant seeds, beginning in our back yards.

Speak directly. "How good is a timely word," says Proverbs 15:23. And how rare! Too often we use language in order to hide. Fear, insecurity and pride cause us to distort and deceive. Authenticity has nothing to hide and everything to give. It can transform how we communicate: evasiveness becomes honest admission of misgivings; excuses become plain confessions of human limitations; sarcastic resentment becomes honest admonition and encouragement; tense misunderstandings give way to hearty laughter; arguments shift from simultaneous monologs to open opportunities to refine opinions and find fresh perspectives. Freed from pride and condemnation we no longer need elaborate justification for our every action, nor careful posturing to protect our fragile image. Humility is freedom; integrity is peace. Authenticity accepts Jesus' simple words: "Let your 'Yes' be 'Yes,' and your 'No,' 'No.' " Foster writes,

> Obey Jesus' instructions about plain, honest speech. "Let what you say be simply 'Yes' or 'No'; anything more than this comes from evil" (Mt. 5:37). If you consent to do a task, do it. Avoid flattery and half-truths. Make honesty and integrity the distinguishing characteristics of your speech. Reject jargon and abstract speculation whose purpose is to obscure and impress rather than to illuminate and inform.[3]

Recovering this idea of plain speech is vital in our age of "doublespeak": to say what we believe in, and to believe in what we say. A timely word is refreshing indeed.

Live wholeheartedly. Our society would allow superficiality to deprive us of true faith, cynicism to deprive us of true hope, and individualism to deprive us of true love. Christ rises in our world and in our lives to restore all three. This is the essence of the abundant life that he promised. Behind all the choices we've explored so far lies this one basic choice: *Do we want the authentic truth of the abundant life or the noisy counterfeit of the junk-filled life?* Our world knows apathy and it knows fanaticism, but this is a third option. To live wholeheartedly is to lay aside all that encumbers us and receive the abundant life with joy. In an age cheapened by superficiality and stress, living the abundant life is to seek to live a life of deep, consistent, trusting, abiding faith; in an age deadened by cynicism and boredom, it is to seek to live a life of honest, intelligent, profound, vibrant hope; in an age isolated by materialism and individualism, it is to seek to live a life of active, overflowing, compassionate, self-giving love.

Wholehearted living is our call as individuals: "Whatever you do, work at it with all your heart, as working for the Lord, not for men" (Col 3:23). "To this end I labor, struggling with all his energy, which so powerfully works in me" (Col 1:29). And it is our calling as the body of Christ:

> Let the peace of Christ rule in your hearts, since as members of one body you were called to peace. And be thankful. Let the word of Christ dwell in you richly as you teach and admonish one another with all wisdom, and as you sing psalms, hymns and spiritual songs with gratitude in your hearts to God. And whatever you do, whether in word or deed, do it all in the name of the Lord Jesus, giving thanks to God the Father through him. (Col 3:15-17)

This thankful, wholehearted living blossoms in exuberance for life and matures into the fruit of sincere joy.

Cut off, we dry up and become brittle. We shuffle through the day, half-asleep as we go about, then toss and turn through the night, half-awake as we sleep. Alone we tend to vacillate between melancholy and flippant sarcasm. But in Christ we are touched by joy. This is why we must reject the simple self-help solutions of Me Generation pop-psychology—they are not wrong, merely inadequate. "Live deliberately, know thyself and to thine own self be true": this is the sum of their counsel, the pursuit of personal happiness. "Live deliberately, know thy God and his intent for thy world and thyself, and to each be true": this is authentic integrity, the key to Christian joy. A profound gap separates the two.

Happiness comes when we find everything going our way;
Joy comes when we find ourselves going God's way.

Happiness sparkles;
Joy glows.

Happiness comes when one of God's good gifts touches our
lives;
Joy comes as a gift when our lives touch God's goodness.

Happiness brightens our day;
Joy lights our way.

Happiness is God's kindness;
Joy is God's grace.

Happiness takes delight in God's presents;
Joy takes delight in God's presence.

Happiness takes in the goodness of the world;
Joy imparts goodness to the world.

Happiness refreshes;
Joy nourishes.

Happiness is grasped in our hands;
Joy grasps our soul.

Happiness is drowned by tears and washed away;
Joy is watered by tears and springs anew.

Happiness comes when we receive a great gift;
Joy comes when we embrace the Great Giver.

Happiness is a life of abundance;
Joy is an abundance of life.

The Chosen Generation

"Do not be afraid. I bring you good news of great joy that will be for all the people." So the angel announced the birth of "Christ the Lord." Sincere joy is contagious. Never existing in isolation, joy is continually reaching outward. The great commandment, "Love the Lord your God with all your heart, soul, mind and strength," always has a second which follows from it, "Love your neighbor as yourself." Jesus told his disciples at the close of his ministry,

As the Father has loved me, so have I loved you. Now remain in my love. If you obey my commands, you will remain in my love, just as I have obeyed my Father's commands and remain in his love. I have told you this so that my joy may be in you and that your joy may be complete. My command is this: Love each other as I have loved you. (Jn 15:9-12)

This was to be their hallmark: "By this all men will know that you are my disciples, if you have love for one another" (Jn 13:35 RSV). The authenticity of our lives authenticates our message. Amidst the cacophony of competing cries we shall have earned the right to be heard. This is the goal of our confrontation with society. Merely bemoaning the waywardness of our world is useless—people have been doing that since ancient Babylon. God is doing amazing things in the world, despite all its corruption. Being caught up in complaining and arguing accomplishes nothing. As Karl Marx aptly pointed out: "The philosophers have only interpreted the world in various ways; the point is to change it." But as Chris-

tians we understand that this must begin with a total transformation of ourselves. This is the climactic "therefore" of Romans 12, which follows Paul's extended explanation of the
new situation brought about by the gospel of Christ:

Therefore, I urge you, brothers, in view of God's mercy, to
offer your bodies as living sacrifices, holy and pleasing to
God—which is your spiritual worship. Do not conform any
longer to the pattern of this world, but be transformed by
the renewing of your mind. Then you will be able to test and
approve what God's will is—his good, pleasing and perfect
will. (Rom 12:1-2)

The result of this radical transformation is a transformed fellowship characterized by sincere love:

Love must be sincere. Hate what is evil; cling to what is
good. Be devoted to one another in brotherly love. Honor
one another above yourselves. Never be lacking in zeal, but
keep your spiritual fervor, serving the Lord. Be joyful in
hope, patient in affliction, faithful in prayer. Share with
God's people who are in need. . . . Live in harmony with
one another. (Rom 12:9-13, 16)

This is the pattern of the kingdom. So often social movements
have the process in reverse: they hope by changing society to
change people. But as C. S. Lewis pointed out, "You can't make
a good omelette from bad eggs." Newspapers filled with tales
of glorious causes degenerating into gory conflicts confirm this.
We must first allow God to renew our worn and weary minds,
and then we can become agents of renewal: first in worn and
weary churches, and then in a worn and weary world. Refined
and molded by his loving touch, we gain the wholeness of
integrity, and that integrity is our peace. And in Christ, personal peace overflows into interpersonal peace

The Hebrews had a word for completeness, *shalom*. Often translated "peace," it refers to completeness, soundness and well-being, a state of concord and harmony. This idea, still a common greeting, was the hope of ancient Israel, finally fulfilled in the Prince of Shalom. He reconciles us first to God (ending our rebellion), then to ourselves (ending our warring double-mindedness), then to our fellow members of his body (ending our estrangement), and only then can we become his agents of reconciliation to our world. This is the sincere piety of humility, not the pompous propriety of Sadducees; this is authentic integrity, not the rigid aloofness of Pharisees. The purpose is not that we may be admired, but that the kingdom may be advanced. Being bearers of shalom is merely being true to our calling:

Therefore, as God's chosen people, holy and dearly loved, clothe yourselves with compassion, kindness, humility, gentleness and patience. Bear with each other and forgive whatever grievances you may have against one another. Forgive as the Lord forgave you. And over all these virtues put on love, which binds them all together in perfect unity.

Let the peace of Christ rule in your hearts, since as members of one body you were called to peace. (Col 3:12-15)

What a tremendous calling we've been given! We set out, not as self-styled reformers, but as "a chosen people, holy and dearly loved." By grace we are a chosen generation, agents of the King, people set apart for a purpose:

You are God's "chosen generation", his "royal priesthood", his "holy nation", his "peculiar people"—all the old titles of God's people now belong to you. It is for you now to demonstrate the goodness of him who has called you out of

darkness into his amazing light. (1 Pet 2:9 Phillips)
This is both a great privilege and a great responsibility. Our task, as Paul sums it up, is this: "Whatever happens, conduct yourselves in a manner worthy of the gospel of Christ" (Phil 1:27). A striking example of this is Paul's own group of associates (the first missionary society) as they crossed borders and cultures with the gospel, their only credentials being lives transformed by the truth. Paul's description of their hope is our goal as well:

> Indeed we want to prove ourselves genuine ministers of God whatever we have to go through . . . with sincerity, with insight and patience; by sheer kindness and the Holy Spirit; with genuine love, speaking the plain truth, and living by the power of God. Our sole defence, our only weapon, is a life of integrity, whether we meet honour or dishonour, praise or blame. (2 Cor 6:4-8 Phillips)

But they weren't exactly always triumphant gospel steamrollers. Instead they were "harassed at every turn" with "conflicts on the outside, fears within" (2 Cor 7:5). We can often expect the same. Yet their weapon of integrity was a powerful one, for amidst their weakness it showed the strength of their message, the power of their God.

When we cease to conform to the forces at work on us from the outside and begin to conform to the masterful hand at work on the inside, then we become lights for a dark world. That world can then see, not just us, but the one who is at work in us. Having seen the gospel, they will be ready to hear the gospel. In a world clamoring for hype, they will have been confronted by the truth.

"Then you will know the truth, and the truth will set you free" (Jn 8:32)—free from all falsity, duplicity and hypocrisy.

"So if the Son sets you free, you will be free indeed" (Jn 8:36). We become whole people, wholeheartedly living the truth. With our hearts and minds, our very lives, transformed, our faith is set free to transform a shackled world. Together, we become bearers of "good tidings of great joy," the contagious community, couriers of the kingdom.

Complete the salvation that God has given you with a proper sense of awe and responsibility. For it is God who is at work within you, giving you the will and the power to achieve his purpose. Do all that you have to do without grumbling or arguing, so that you may be blameless and harmless, faultless children of God, living in a warped and diseased age, and shining like lights in a dark world. For you hold up in your hands the very word of life. (Phil 2:12-16 Phillips)

Notes

Chapter 1: Welcome to the World
[1]Eugene Peterson, *A Long Obedience in the Same Direction* (Downers Grove, Ill.: InterVarsity Press, 1980), p. 11.
[2]Eugene Peterson, *Run with the Horses* (Downers Grove, Ill.: InterVarsity Press, 1983), p. 136.

Chapter 2: The Junk Generation
[1]Bruce Lockerbie, "Could 25 Billion Hamburgers Be Wrong?" *HIS Magazine,* April 1978.
[2]Peterson, *Long Obedience,* pp. 11-12.
[3]Alvin Toffler, *Future Shock* (New York: Random House, 1970), p. 88.

Chapter 3: The Me Generation
[1]Philip Slater, *The Pursuit of Loneliness* (Boston: Beacon Press, 1970) pp. 7-8.
[2]Tom Howard, *Chance or Dance* (Wheaton, Ill.: Harold Shaw Publishers, 1972), p. 104; quoted in Peterson, *Run with the Horses,* p. 11.
[3]From notes I took at lecture series given by Robert Bellah.
[4]Quoted in Charles Swindoll, *Strengthening Your Grip* (Waco, Tex.: Word, 1982), p. 29.
[5]Ibid., p. 37.
[6]Alan Loy McGinnis, *The Friendship Factor* (Minneapolis: Augsburg, 1979), p.

42.

[7]Swindoll, *Strengthening Your Grip*, p. 29.

[8]J. C. Wynn, *Family Therapy in Pastoral Ministry* (San Francisco: Harper & Row, 1982), p. 14.

[9]Joan Wulff, "Searching for Community," *HIS Magazine*, March 1982, p. 4.

Chapter 4: The Cluttered Generation

[1]Arthur G. Gish, *Beyond the Rat Race* (New Canaan, Conn.: Keats, 1973), p. 21.

[2]Vernard Eller, *The Mad Morality or the Ten Commandments Revisited* (New York: Abingdon, 1970), p. 70; quoted in Ronald J. Sider, *Rich Christians in an Age of Hunger* (Downers Grove, Ill.: InterVarsity Press, 1977), p. 48.

[3]Sider, *Rich Christians*, pp. 47-48.

[4]Dietrich Bonhoeffer, *The Cost of Discipleship* (New York: Macmillan, 1963), p. 197.

[5]Kahlil Gibran, *The Prophet* (New York: Alfred A. Knopf, 1971), p. 19.

[6]Quoted in Daniel Webster, *Christian Living in a Pagan Culture* (Wheaton, Ill.: Tyndale House, 1980), p. 59.

[7]Ibid., p. 32.

[8]Quoted in ibid., p. 105.

[9]Ibid., p. 106.

[10]Bonhoeffer, *The Cost of Discipleship*, p. 194.

[11]Richard Foster, *Celebration of Discipline* (San Francisco: Harper & Row, 1978), p. 77.

[12]Donald L. Bubna and Sarah Ricketts, *Building People through Sharing Caring Fellowship* (Wheaton, Ill.: Tyndale, 1978), p. 54.

[13]Gibran, *The Prophet*, p. 20.

Chapter 5: The Frantic Generation

[1]Foster, *Celebration of Discipline*, p. 70.

[2]Quoted in Keith Miller, *Habitation of Dragons* (Waco, Tex.: Word, 1980), p. 56.

[3]Foster, *Celebration of Discipline*, p. 84.

[4]Henry David Thoreau, *Walden* (Boston: Houghton Mifflin, 1899), p. 10.

[5]Foster, *Celebration of Discipline*, p. 20.

Chapter 6:The Restless Generation

[1]Jacques Ellul, quoted in Peterson, *Long Obedience*, p. 100.

[2]Robert Lee, quoted in Ted W. Engstrom and Alex MacKenzie, *Managing Your Time* (Grand Rapids, Mich.: Zondervan, 1968).

[3]Foster, *Celebration of Discipline*, p. 166.

[4]Tom Sine, *The Mustard Seed Conspiracy* (Waco, Tex.: Word, 1981), p. 116.

[5]Ibid.

[6]Foster, *Celebration of Discipline,* p. 1.

[7]C. S. Lewis, *Prince Caspian* (New York: Macmillan, 1978), p. 136.

Chapter 7: The Hollow Generation

[1]Michael Green, *Running from Reality* (Downers Grove, Ill.: InterVarsity Press, 1983), p. 66.

[2]Os Guinness, *The Gravedigger File* (Downers Grove, Ill.: InterVarsity Press, 1983), p. 233.

[3]Green, *Running from Reality,* p. 11.

[4]Sine, *Mustard Seed Conspiracy,* pp. 235-36.

[5]Jacques Rossel, *Mission in a Dynamic Society* (London: SCM Press, 1968), p. 133.

[6]C. S. Lewis, *Mere Christianity* (New York: Macmillan, 1978), p. 106.

[7]C. S. Lewis, *The Four Loves* (New York: Harcourt Brace Jovanovich, 1960), p. 169.

Chapter 8: Couriers of the Kingdom

[1]Peterson, *Run with the Horses,* pp. 11-12.

[2]Dietrich Bonhoeffer, *Ethics* (New York: Macmillan, 1955), p. 68.

[3]Foster, *Celebration of Discipline,* p. 81.